T0267480

FIVE TRIPS

FIVE TRIPS

AN INVESTIGATIVE JOURNEY INTO MENTAL HEALTH, PSYCHEDELIC HEALING, AND SAVING A LIFE

KENDIS GIBSON

A POST HILL PRESS BOOK

Five Trips:
An Investigative Journey into Mental Health, Psychedelic Healing, and Saving a Life

ISBN: 979-8-88845-642-2
ISBN (eBook): 979-8-88845-643-9

Cover design by Conroy Accord
Cover photo by Mark Leibowitz
Interior design and composition by Greg Johnson, Textbook Perfect

Post Hill Press
New York • Nashville
posthillpress.com

Published in the United States of America
1 2 3 4 5 6 7 8 9 10

To my mom and dad

Contents

Preface

As I sat down to write this book, I realized this journey would be the most difficult thing I've ever written, recounted, and revealed. Yes, this story revolves around depression, extremely deep suicidal depression (think "drinking bottles of wine while The Carpenters lull you to sleep just moments before you can consume several sleeping pills sitting in the palm of your hand" type of desolation). But this is also a funny, uplifting story. If you've ever met me or seen me on television, you know I'm a humorous, snarky, sarcastic, and positive person. You'll definitely see that in this book, but you'll also learn about the parts that even my immediate family members and some of my closest friends are unaware of. The story will take you behind the scenes of my career highlights, including being granted rare interviews with Beyoncé on numerous occasions, and being the first English-language American network journalist to discover Colombian singer-songwriter Maluma.

After decades of dealing with depression due to a myriad of reasons, including childhood sexual abuse, losing and discovering the body of my first love days after our initial kiss, and years of mental shrapnel from being on the front lines of the saddest news stories, I was able to find solutions. For several of the most challenging experiences—five, precisely—that drove me to suicidal ideation,

I found various successful answers. Not therapy, not prescription medicine, not Jesus, not meditation. I found solutions by turning to illegal drugs.

Psychedelics (except for ketamine) are classified as Schedule 1 drugs in the United States. Possession of certain amounts of psychedelics can result in felony charges, similar to heroin, and result in up to thirty years behind bars. As a national news anchor and reporter, I didn't partake lightly but out of necessity. At several points in my life, it was either die by suicide or try to find answers with some form of hallucinogen. I spent five years—and strained my savings—traveling the world, experiencing different forms of psychedelics, and speaking with various leading voices in the field. With each journey and trip, I kept discovering something new that brought healing to my heart, body, and soul. However, in no way am I presenting this as something everyone battling with mental health issues and/or PTSD should do; I'm simply recounting how they helped me with particular struggles in my own life.

A warning about this book: it deals with heavy subject matter, and often in graphic detail. It recounts, in raw fashion, some very personal trials and tribulations, and I would be lying if I didn't admit my reluctance to retell these episodes in some form or fashion. I wondered, *Am I sharing too much? What will my new employers think? What will my family think? What about my abusers?* In the end, I realized I needed to go on this journey and take readers along with me, and here's why.

So many people have suffered some form of trauma, whether its abuse, tragic deaths, depression, or racial hostility. I can go on with the types. When I had some of my first positive psychedelic experiences and started observing the positive changes in myself, I started reading some of the leading books on psychedelics. Michael Pollan's *How to Change Your Mind* is considered the gold standard for many, as it dives deep into the science and research. I read James Fadiman's

The Psychedelic Explorer's Guide, which chronicled his more than forty-year experience in psychedelics and laid out best practices for safe hallucinogenic journeys. But the majority of experts who wrote or were cited in these books were White men, i.e., the stereotype I associate with the psychedelic movement.

While all these books were informative and well researched, I did not see myself in their pages. I had a difficult time equating my story as a Black man with those of the White experts, and it was hard to connect my life experience with theirs. As I penned this book, I sought out everyone from the average plant medicine connoisseur to scientists and doctors who are working at the top tiers of this industry, and I discovered something interesting: the vast majority are people of color. Not only did I find there are countless BIPOC experts in this field, but I was also amazed and heartened to discover plant medicine's deep ancestral therapeutic roots among people of color.

And there's one more thing before we get started. There's an old quote, occasionally attributed to Ralph Waldo Emerson, saying, "Life is about the journey, not the destination. We won't truly know the journey until we've taken it." I think that saying epitomizes my journey, which, at times, felt like a global road trip. I took many exits and met many colorful and smart characters along the way. I had unexpected and unplanned experiences until I arrived at my "destination." I'll admit that ultimately, it may require some readers to suspend disbelief a bit in what we see and sense every day in order to embrace my truth.

INTRODUCTION

Empire State of Mind

The things that go through your mind as you're about to kill yourself are pretty interesting. My thoughts ran the gamut. *Did I prepare my will? Should I have left a note behind? What will my funeral look like, and who will attend? Also, did I flush the toilet after I pissed for the last time?* The idea of someone walking into the apartment after I was gone and finding the place wasn't tidy horrified me. Not to mention, I was concerned about the mess my brain matter would leave on the sidewalk down below.

No one ever said being suicidal was a rational state of mind.

This, however, was my mindset in October 2018 as I prepared to dangle from the twelfth story of my Manhattan high-rise, convinced this would be the end. Getting to this point, on the brink of my death, was the culmination of a mission that began as adulthood peaked and never relented. I figured it was my destiny to die at a relatively young age.

There was nothing special about October 12. No reason that day was meant to be my last. I had just anchored the early-morning newscast as usual. I left ABC's Studio 3A, grabbed a taxicab for the short ride home, kissed my partner of nearly a decade goodnight, and crawled into bed as he left for work. A few hours later, I woke up, drugged on two Ambien tablets, and walked into the kitchen. I texted a friend to let her know I had prepared everything for this day, including filing my will and preparing my funeral. I ended the message by telling her I felt at peace.

This drug-fueled suicidal mindset was strangely orgasmic. It was as if my lifelong struggle with depression had been one long edging session, and this would be the climax. And why not now? I was at the height of my career, anchoring a popular network morning newscast. I had a beautiful apartment in New York City and was dating a gorgeous blue-eyed White guy, so I was basically living the "American dream."

I walked through the kitchen, stopping at the refrigerator to grab some leftover cheesecake, customary for me on those Ambien trips, and proceeded to the window ledge. The cool early autumn air did little to wake me from my haze as I opened the window. The city skyline had the aspect of a real-life Instagram filter, with spectacularly spellbinding blue skies. I slowly reached the ledge, put my left foot over it, followed seconds later by my right foot, and grabbed onto the glass above me, my fingers going pale from pressing so tightly. Tears filled my eyes as I reviewed my end-of-life to-do list one more time before I committed to jumping onto a metro bus below.

I prepared to let go of the ledge. My fingers were already numb from the effort of holding on. I was ready to plummet to my death.

What a life I had lived, born in poverty in the Caribbean, growing up without television, immigrating to the United States, assimilating in whatever way I could, and joining the TV industry, achieving fame and fortune. But it was never enough to quell the darkness that had lived within me for almost as long as I could remember.

CHAPTER 1

Belize

I was born in Belize, the bite-sized country nestled next to Mexico and Guatemala and one of only two countries in Latin America where English is the official language. The country has been described as a Caribbean island that got lost at sea, and then got shipwrecked into the Central American coast. I spent my first five years living in a tiny, dilapidated two-story house with blue tarps covering the holes in the tin roof. My mom would never admit it, but I'm confident I was an accident. She was thirty-six years old when she had me, and giving birth at that age in a country with limited medical facilities was considered highly risky. Plus, my parents didn't need another child, especially another boy. After all, they already had six sons: Alrick Jr., Dean, Brian, Aldoray, Brent, and Marvin. My mom was confident she was pregnant with a girl while carrying me. She had picked out the name Kendra and was forced to go with a made-up variation of that name, Kendis, when I made my appearance.

"Another one," my mother exclaimed as this bawling, already balding, oversize baby boy (me) emerged. "Well, I be one eye be bwoy, I nuh believe dis, wow," my mom recalled telling the doctor. I still have no idea what she meant, but it certainly didn't sound like excitement. A girl was the only thing she had prayed for and asked the "good Lord" to deliver. Little did she realize she had packed her baby girl in her last baby boy.

With its four small bedrooms, our house needed to be bigger to sleep four people, much less nine of us. Three bedrooms were on the second floor, but my brother Aldoray was in the one above our kitchen, which I sometimes shared as well. Aldoray's bed was up against a wall, and its height lined up seamlessly with the bottom of a windowsill. We didn't have air-conditioning and probably didn't even know it existed. We didn't have fans because we couldn't afford them, and the country's frequent blackouts rendered them useless. To cool off at night, we just slept with the windows open and prayed we didn't get bitten up by the mosquitoes.

Kids in Belize didn't routinely sleep in cribs, and there was no room in my parents' bed, as they were increasingly growing (horizontally, not vertically). I was shy of six months old and sleeping in Aldoray's bed one night, but I kept getting pushed toward the open window. I eventually rolled over a few times and rolled right out of the window, plummeting two floors to the ground below. Apparently, some of my brothers heard my ear-piercing screams but ignored them for an hour until they couldn't stand the sound of my cries. "Da weh Kendis?" Aldoray asked as he walked around the house with a flashlight since the lights had gone out thanks to yet another power outage.

Aldoray suspected I had somehow ended up outside, but he searched the front yard. Once he doubled back to his bedroom, he finally thought to look out his window to the ground below. My big, white eyes appeared amid a sea of darkness. I had fallen into a life-saving pile of leftover food, dishwater, and trash. We didn't have indoor plumbing or a garbage disposal; everything was tossed through the kitchen window below my brother's bedroom. Over the years, that mix of dishwater, chicken bones, rice and beans, and everything not consumed at the dinner table gathered outside that kitchen window. The massive pile of waste cushioned my fall and saved my life.

Strangely, I never realized how incredibly poor we were during my childhood. Perhaps it was because we could afford someone to pick up our shit from the outhouse. Most homes in Belize had outhouses; my family had a wooden one just a few steps away from our open-air vat, the primary source of fresh drinking water. In some societies, having an expensive Rolex or a luxurious car symbolized wealth; for my family in Belize, it was the nightly visits from Ms. Cynthia. I watched as she walked into our front yard wearing no gloves and grabbed the handle of the dingy white toilet bucket from our outhouse. Without much thought, she grabbed the bucket, occasionally put the lid on, and slowly walked through our yard, her body tilting to the opposite side of the bucket, depending on whether it was a heavy flow day for my family. She would make the two-block walk to the downtown canal—usually accompanied by others doing this walk of shame—to dump the waste into our country's elaborate outdoor sewage system. It would be decades before the government invested in more septic tanks.

Despite being able to have the services of Ms. Cynthia, we couldn't afford much more else, including health care. One time, I sliced open my foot with a broken beer bottle when I was just three or four, but there was no hospital visit. We had to pray for the best and hope it healed without infection. Praying, hoping, and traditional medicine kept us alive, but home remedies couldn't cure everything, especially tapeworms. My brothers and I had tapeworms all the time, and nothing could ever get rid of them completely. Marvin had the worst experience. He was twelve years old when he started coughing at the dining table one night, seemingly unable to breathe. At one point, my mom thought maybe he was choking on a piece of food, so she performed the Belizean Heimlich maneuver. She pounded the crap out of his back, trying to dislodge whatever he seemed to be choking on. I was across the table, horrified yet curious about what was happening.

Marvin kept choking, and then he placed both hands around his throat and squeezed as he gagged and gasped for breath. I didn't understand why he was squeezing his own throat if he couldn't breathe, but then again, I didn't understand how my mom's pounding on his back was helping matters either. Just as Marvin was about to pass out, his body convulsing, he reached into his own mouth with one hand as if he could dislodge whatever was blocking his windpipe. Within seconds he withdrew his hand and with it, a slimy, thick, pale-yellow tapeworm over ten inches long. His eyes widened, bloodshot and teary, a mix of shock and disgust crossing his face as he looked at the wiggling worm. My mom stopped beating his back and ran to the other side of the room in horror. The contrasting image of his dark, Caribbean sun-drenched skin and this squiggly, pale, flapping monster from the deep remains etched in my brain to this day, and in our family Marvin is still referred to as Medusa Marv.

Moving On Up

I knew I was different early on, but I never understood why. I loved *I Dream of Jeannie* because of Jeannie's belly-button-baring midriff and those puffy chiffon pants. I was fascinated by pageant queens, and I'd feel the urge to bury my face in the armpits of boys. The signals were always there, but it took me years to come to terms with them. Several factors contributed to my hesitation, including my family's strict adherence to an oppressive form of Christianity. We attended Wesley Methodist Church in downtown Belize City every Sunday. And despite my best efforts at faking being sick, Sunday school was mandatory. We had weekly prayer meetings, and each school day started with a prayer. My parents even selected a deacon from the church to be my godfather. At the earliest inkling that I might be a big homo, my mom imparted, "Jesus would rather me be dead than have a son who was gay."

Still, my early years spent living in that old house, with an outdoor toilet, Medusa Marv, and sleeping all on top of each other were among the happiest of my life. With every ladder of success climbed, my hold on happiness loosened considerably. That pattern started when we moved to a brand-new home on the city's west side. In Belize, the farther you get away from the sea, where the potential for a hurricane to destroy your home was greater, the more elevated your social status. Like George Jefferson, we were moving on up.

Our new house was a large two-story structure built from the ground up by my dad. The bottom floor was an all-concrete space my dad planned to turn into a bakery or a furniture store. For some reason, neither came to fruition. The upstairs was an all-wooden frame house, which was our living quarters. Everything in the house was so new and fancy by Belize standards that we felt like we had made it to the big time. I mean, we even had a septic tank. What says high status in Belize more than saying goodbye to your outhouse?

The family room in the front of our house led to a concrete veranda with views of the neighbors' homes and the street below. On most nights, whatever was popping off in the streets would be the extent of our family's entertainment. We had a massive nineteen-inch color television that my dad bought on one of his trips to the United States and drove three thousand miles back to Belize. But we couldn't watch anything because Belize didn't have a single TV station at that time. That television became a pretty useless piece of furniture, except when we used it to play video games on cassettes shipped from the U.S. that we had to borrow from our friends.

My mom was happy with the house because she had a brand-new kitchen for all her needs. Water flowed through an indoor faucet. There was still no dishwasher, but at least there was no longer the need to toss wastewater or food out the back window on most days. Sometimes my mom still threw food out the window, but that was only to feed the resilient little stray dog, Blackie, who adopted our family (probably because of the scraps she fed him).

Upstairs, there were three bedrooms lined against one side of the building. My parents' bedroom was at the front of the house, my oldest brothers' was at the rear, and the room I shared with some of my other brothers and another teenage relative was in the middle. Our room had three beds, including a bunk bed and one for my teenage relative. Al had his twin bed once again adjacent to the window, similar to the one I fell out of at our last house. I was so excited to have a bed to myself, I created my sanctuary on that bottom bunk with photos of Michael Jackson, Bob Marley, and Queen Elizabeth taped up on the wall. I loved spending time in my semi-gay sanctuary, but it soon became my torture chamber.

Waking Nightmare

My sixth birthday stands as a pivotal moment in that house. It was the first time I was celebrated with a real party, with a cake, a clown, and all my cousins in attendance. And it was also the first night I was raped by my teenage relative..

I was fast asleep when I heard and soon felt movement from the bunk bed above me. My relative quietly climbed down the steps from his bunk, but instead of heading to the bathroom as usual, this time was different. He slowly crawled onto the foot of my bed. As he inched his way up to my side, the mattress sank slightly lower with each move, and finally he pressed his teenage body behind me, whispering "shhh" in my ear. Aldoray was asleep less than six feet away. Back then, I slept in full pajamas, as many kids did, despite the warm nighttime temperatures. My pajama bottom got slowly pulled from my foot down and off, and my mouth was pried open and stuffed with a portion of those pants.

I had no idea what was happening as he started penetrating me. There was no substance to ease the physical pain, just a cloth in my mouth to quiet this child from screaming in excruciating pain from what was occurring. It was probably a relatively quick experience, but it seemed to last several hours. It would take decades for me to reconcile that this was my first sexual experience and to grasp that it was at such a tender age and by a family member. I tried to mumble questions to ask what happened, but he only whispered, "Be quiet." He crawled back up the side ladder, and within minutes he was snoring as if nothing had transpired. My pajamas were still stuffed solidly in my mouth; my eyes began to well up from the pulsating pain in my butt. I couldn't fall asleep that night.

The following day at school was just as painful. Trying to sit in class for eight hours was excruciating. The entire day, I couldn't sit still because of the pain and asked if I could stand in a corner. My parochial corporal punishment school saw that as disobedience, and my teacher ordered ten hand lashings. The anal bleeding lasted several days, even after the pain subsided. While I was too young to come to terms with what took place, I was well aware of the traumatizing fallout from the abuse—and it was not the end.

I was still not fully healed when it happened again one week later. My relative quietly crawled down the steps to my lower bunk bed again. He pulled down my Flintstones underwear and, again without mercy, penetrated me violently and repeatedly for several minutes. This time, his hands were over my mouth instead of the pajamas to prevent me from making noise. I tried fighting back because I was still very much sore. While my comprehension of what was taking place didn't increase this second time, I knew enough that the pain was too much for me to handle. Despite his hands covering my mouth, I kept making noises, hoping he would stop. After several minutes, he stopped, slowly pulled away from me, and crawled back to his bunk. He was again asleep and snoring within a few minutes while I suffered another restless night.

I tried different tactics to repel his advances as the weeks and months went on. I pretended to be asleep on other occasions, but in the end, it didn't matter if I was awake. My body was just a vessel for him. I dreaded the nights my brother Al stayed over at his girlfriend's place, because it meant the sessions would last longer, and any noises I made were in a vacuum. My abusive relative usually sat across from me at the breakfast table and pretended the previous night's assault was a figment of my imagination.

The assaults continued every week for nearly a year. I never told my parents or brothers what was taking place. As a six-year-old going on seven, how exactly do you explain this? I assumed it was a normal part of childhood. Finally, I became frustrated by the unrelenting attacks and decided to resist his assaults. One night, Aldoray was in bed when my teenage relative crawled down from his bed and began the formulaic process. By this point, he had stopped stuffing my mouth with my clothes or covering it with his hand. As he started to rape me, I screamed "no" at the top of my lungs—loud enough that I figured Aldoray would hear it, wake up, and come to my rescue. My scream immediately forced him to back off and quietly rush to his bunk.

Back then, my bawling didn't immediately wake Al, nor did my screams of "no." But it was enough to scare my rapist into stopping the assault that night, and eventually he permanently cut out the behavior. Each subsequent evening and for weeks, I would go to bed dreading it would happen again and resiliently contemplate how I would stop the next assault. Eventually, he found a young neighborhood girl to date, and I realized the assaults would never happen again. Perhaps it was a version of Stockholm syndrome, but I was somewhat jealous of his new girlfriend. I started to wish it could all happen again, and one night I even crawled up to his bunk bed to try to instigate the action. In hindsight, I'm happy he never did it again, but I believe this was when my sleeping issues began.

He went on to marry that girlfriend and have several children with her. To this day, I've never confronted him about it. And perhaps it eventually contributed to us having the least cordial relationship among my relatives. I fear that by not speaking up, it may have happened with others over the years. Or perhaps it was a crime of convenience in a country where any sexual proclivity could get you shunned by the church.

Indeed, it was not easy to be gay, lesbian, or bisexual in Belize. In section 53 of Belize's constitution, drafted in 1981, homosexuality was officially outlawed by using an old British colonial rule that banned "carnal intercourse against the order of nature." As such, it made sexual relationships between adult men, even within the confines of their own homes, illegal and punishable by death. The architect of section 53 and much of the constitution was the father of the country, George Price. He was a successful politician who lived to age ninety-two, never had a female companion, never married, and never had any children. But Belizeans didn't need a law on the books to make them homophobic then. It was part of the country's—and much of the Caribbean's—culture. Beyond my parents constantly bashing their swishy son for his ways, kids in school would often call me a "batty man" as they beat me in schoolyards or on my walk home most days. In Belizean Creole, the word "batty" refers to your butt. And if you were a "batty man," it meant you liked butt sex with other men.

The term was used as a slur against many as they were beaten and, in some cases, killed for being gay in the country. But as was evident from my own experience in my household, plenty of so-called batty men lived on the down-low. Belizeans would sing patriotic songs, including one for the biggest holiday of the year on the tenth of September, St. George's Caye Day. It recalls a famed battle fought by the British colonialists against other invaders from Spain. To commemorate the day, we were all taught a catchy song that recounts the struggle at St. George's Caye on September 10, 1798. However, the hook for that song had an unsavory gay-bashing line at the end. Everywhere we celebrated the holiday, people would scream at the top of their lungs, "Hip hip hooray," followed by the homophobic trope "yuh batty gay." In short, it was as inhospitable an environment in which to grapple with my sexuality as any you could imagine.

A Boy Named Manny

Perhaps it was my discomfort with my sexuality or my childhood introversion, but I didn't have a lot of friends. At my first home in the alley, most of the kids I played around with were cousins who lived in our massive family compound. My days at school were spent fighting bullies due to my sexuality but also because of my relative smarts. I'm not saying I was a genius, but I did skip two grades and was not too modest to remind classmates about it. At home, despite having so many siblings, I always felt like I grew up as an only child because there were nine years between me and my next youngest brother, Marvin.

I slowly made friends in the new Lake Independence neighborhood. I attended parentally mandated Sunday service every week and found some friends in church school there, but little did I realize the one person I would hit it off with was right across the street. I was about eight when I got my first bicycle as a Christmas gift. I had no idea how to ride the bike, and my parents spent hours one late afternoon chasing after me, trying to teach me. I was alone just as they were about to give up on me getting the hang of it.

I rode without anyone holding on to the back of the seat and started peddling rapidly with the biggest grin. That smile reflected my incomparable feeling of joy and freedom as I rode down Santa Barbara Street and briefly looked back at my parents, who had let go. I was so excited I paid no attention to what was ahead of me, which turned out to be my neighbor Manuel, who couldn't avoid my erratic bicycling. I ran straight into him. We both crashed into the rusty-colored dirt road. I had met Manny, his mom, and his brother before, but we had never hung out as we attended different schools and churches. I got up and said, "Why are you going to run into me like that?"—an aggressive accusation he didn't take too kindly to. "What are you talking about?" he responded. "I was walking on the street and you made me run all over the road to avoid you on your cheap bike." Until he pointed it out, I thought I was riding a rather expensive BMX bike, but the fake BMX sticker peeled off in the crash.

I was too embarrassed for myself and my parents to admit the bike was a cheap rip-off of the expensive bikes we had only heard about, so I said, "Boi, sorry," picked up my ride, and walked back to my house, my head firmly lowered in shame, but also a bit of intrigue. Manuel was my age and probably some sort of Latino mix, as is customary in Belize. He was a skinny kid and unusually tall for an eight-year-old, nearly five feet, with long black hair just a few inches shy of his shoulders and the most beautiful smile. He was your typical Belizean Blatino blend that didn't speak Spanish but had all the blessings of mixed-race features.

I didn't understand my emotions whenever I saw Manny, but I knew they were honest and fantastic. I experienced tingling, hair-raising goose bumps and a high heart rate whenever I saw him. I am fairly sure he felt dread at the sight of me. We were too young to know about girls, sexuality, or our desires, but whenever I saw him, I had a rush of emotions I had never experienced or could comprehend.

Manny had lived in the neighborhood years before my family arrived, but there was rarely an opportunity to see or interact with him. I was so happy that my bike-riding skills inadvertently forced us into a friendship. We started spending many post-school afternoons in his and his brother's bedroom, playing on the streets with our bikes and doing the old-fashioned paddling of tires with a stick while running behind them. One of our favorite things was walking about a half mile from the house down this long dirt path lined with thick forest, often a dumping ground for people's trash toward the Belize River. Like a scene out of *Stand By Me*, we would walk to the river with his brother and a couple of other neighborhood kids, skip rocks, chill by the water, and have the sort of deep discussions you'd expect eight-year-olds in Belize to have. That trail through the woods to the river was our favorite hangout area as kids in that neighborhood because it was remote enough to provide a jungle escape from our homes and parents yet just a mile away and easily accessible by foot. And despite all the broken glass and debris on the trail, we often made it to the river barefoot. We had plenty of shoes back home, but running barefoot felt more natural.

Our nights in Belize were spent sitting with our family, eating dinner, playing card games, or listening to the radio. Our school didn't emphasize homework, so we rarely had that to occupy our time. The country would often suffer blackouts, so we didn't spend too many nights up late. Manny and I would occasionally play along with his brother well past nightfall until the blackouts made it impossible to see our own hands, much less each other. And unlike in the United States, sleepovers weren't common, and not with someone who lived across the street. Yet, as my fascination with Manny grew, I knew I wanted to spend an overnight with him, perhaps hoping to do the same thing my relative did with me a few years earlier. Whatever that was.

One evening after dinner, after a blackout hit Belize City, I told my mom and dad I would head over to Manny's place to hang out with him and his younger brother. I crossed the street in the dark and walked upstairs to their candlelit second-floor apartment. Although their home had candles burning, many in the country often waited out the blackouts by sitting around in the dark, using it as an opportunity for conversation. However, I used this blackout as a chance to spend time with Manny. It turned out that evening's blackout lasted for several hours, well beyond what would normally be our bedtime. His mom decided to go to bed early along with his younger brother, with whom he shared a bunk bed but that night decided to crash in his mom's room. His mom made a deal with us that we could stay up, but the candles would have to be out.

Manny and I never had a romantic vibe, but I certainly had feelings for him. I was still too young to understand what those emotions meant and scarred from physical interaction with any other person, especially another male. But there was something about the energy of that evening that made me feel something would happen, so I was in no rush to go home. After hanging in the dark and talking briefly, we decided to head to the kid's bedroom at the front of the house, where the moon provided a touch of lighting. I figured I would spend the night at Manny's and see how things developed. The two of us lay down next to each other with our heads buttressed against each other. Our arms were so close that I was fairly sure he could feel the goose bumps. My heart raced so hard whenever we stopped talking; I was sure he could hear the loud, rapid beating. I was sure Manny was into girls, even though he had not interacted romantically with them. We used to talk about the girls in his class he had crushes on, and I would pretend to have similar feelings. Still, I felt confident I could hold his hand, so I went for it, using my right pinkie finger to test the waters and perhaps be the sacrificial lamb if my advance was rebuffed.

My pinkie twitched his finger, and much to my excitement, both hooked on to each other. I slowly moved the others into the fold of his left hand, and before I knew it, we were holding hands and slowly started squeezing each other's hands. At that moment, an overwhelming thought came over me: *What the hell am I supposed to do next?* It was equally new to Manny, because clearly he didn't know what to do next or what to make of the events either. We fell asleep for a bit, holding each other's hands tightly when, finally, the lights came back on and woke us up. I decided to get ready to go home to bed but wondered if I would ever have this opportunity again. With my heart palpitations rapidly increasing, we were both staring at the bed bunk above us when I offered the disclaimer, "I don't know what I'm doing or what we did, but I hope it's okay." After disavowing responsibility for my actions, I slowly lifted my head and hovered my face over Manny's, who had his eyes wide open. I lowered my lips onto his and slowly kissed him. I made the weird smooching sound I'd heard people make in the movies when they kiss each other. Both our eyes remained open as we moved our lips around in the awkward dance you'd expect from two people who didn't know what they were doing. Those goose bumps initially triggered by my excitement returned over the seconds-long kiss that felt like a lifetime. I've experienced the emotions I had during this first kiss only twice in my life: that moment with Manny and when I won my first Emmy Award more than a decade later.

As quickly as it started, it was over. I pulled my lips away from Manny's and continued to stare into his eyes. I assumed all that tingling that vibrated through my body was love. Manny kept to the same stone-faced look he had even when we were lip-locked. I couldn't tell if he wanted to kiss more, hug, or throw up, as his face showed no emotions. Finally, after a few more seconds, he said, "Dat mih nice," which allowed me to be relieved and warmed my heart and everything in my body. "Good evening," which for us meant good night, and I got up to leave, at which point he grabbed and hugged me tightly in his arms. In some strange way, it hearkened back to thoughts of my relative attacking me a few years earlier. But for the first time, I realized there could be a positive interaction in bed with another human.

Before heading home, I jumped out of bed and briefly looked back at Manny. I had no idea this would be the last time I saw him. I ran across the street and tiptoed into our house, only to realize my dad was still awake playing solitaire. My dad always had sleeping problems, an unfortunate trait passed down to a couple of my siblings and me. It was well past midnight on a school night, so I ran straight into my bedroom, but I couldn't sleep. I kept replaying it in my head every second of the night, and with each rerun, the smile on my face grew even bigger. My internal conversation at the time ran the gamut. *What are these feelings? Does it mean we are dating? Is this what love feels like? Oh shit, am I now a batty man?* The questions did nothing to quell my excitement.

That night was the first time I wrote down my thoughts. I pulled out the pages at the back of a textbook and started writing down my feelings and hopeful thoughts for our future. I guess it was a diary, but I didn't even know what that was. I just wanted to commemorate the moment somehow in my most beautiful cursive writing. The only thing that could get me to sleep was the thought that the quicker I passed out, the sooner I would wake up and be able to see Manny. I thought perhaps I'd see him early before we both went to our respective schools in the morning. I knew for sure we'd see each other at night, and God willing, we would have another country-wide blackout, and I'd have an excuse to sneak across the street and cuddle with Manny. I've rarely gone to sleep so happy to be alive.

The next day was Wednesday. I'm not entirely sure why I remembered that little nugget. Perhaps because I thought it would be a day that would build on the previous day's excitement. Little did I know, as I woke up that morning with a glow still on my face, that I'd eventually remember that day for all the wrong reasons. As I left my house, my school uniform seemed extra crisp and white. I looked over to Manny's house, but the kids' bedroom curtain seemed unmoved from when I'd left, and there were no signs of him or his mom and brother.

I walked to school with some pep and could barely concentrate on the lessons. I rushed back home and looked again at Manny's place as I entered my house, but there was no sign of anyone. I didn't think anything of it; even in hindsight, there wasn't much to take away. Manny and his brother weren't out that Wednesday evening playing, as was usually the case, and the lights were not on at their home. My family and I spent a reasonably mundane evening under the lights as there were no blackouts, but you would have thought differently when looking at Manny's home. The lights didn't appear on all night.

The next day, I glanced over as I headed out to school and again didn't see any activity. I went to Manny's and knocked on his apartment door that evening to hang out with him. It turned out his mom and brother had been home but were spending most of their time in the back living and bedrooms of the house. "Good night, Ms. Gloria," I greeted her in the traditional way. "Amih dih look fuh Manny."

"It nuh deh home. Ih mih gone since yesterday," his mom said, which was the first time I learned that he had been missing since Wednesday morning when he went to school. His mom and brother didn't seem concerned about it, so I assumed he had gone to see a grandparent or other family member.

When I went by Manny's home the following day, his mom once again said he wasn't there. Again, she seemed only mildly concerned, but my concern grew this time because other family members at the house hadn't heard from him either. That evening, I told my parents he was missing, and that news also was met with an equal lack of concern. I, on the other hand, had an elevated level of angst because of what happened during our previous interaction. And then that Friday, my mom told me that Manny's mom had called the police to investigate his disappearance. I didn't go to their apartment that afternoon, because it seemed like the disappearance had finally taken on an uncomfortable level of despair.

Over the weekend, there was no increased police activity or search party gatherings. His family probably assumed he had run off and would eventually return. I started panicking that my actions forced him to run away. I may have been one of the last people to see Manny, and one of the last actions he made before running off was something that he didn't necessarily want to do. I relived those seconds we'd spent in bed, but with a different scope. Was he staring at me while we were kissing because he was experiencing inner turmoil about what was happening? By advancing on him, did I assault him just like my relative had done to me years earlier?

I was increasingly filled with stress and guilt. I rode my bike to my *Stand By Me* trail through the nearby trees to chill by the river and clear my head. It was a beautiful sunny and typically hot and humid Caribbean day, but the emerald-green Belize River was a little swollen beyond the banks following several days of rain. The heavy downpour brought a lot of trees and debris from upriver, which is why I didn't make much of the toy doll I saw trapped in a tree branch about ten feet out in the middle of the river. The doll had a clenched fist in the air; the rest of the object was below the waterline. The more I stared at it, though, the more it didn't add up. What kind of doll is so pale white and has a clenched fist? At no point did I fathom that object could have been Manny, but I still rode my bike straight to his mom's place.

When I walked in and approached his mom in the kitchen, she was surrounded by family members. "Ms. Gloria, I was at the river, and I saw a doll in the water, but it didn't look like a normal doll.

It may be Manny in the water," I told his mom. Even as the words came out of my mouth and I told her that I suspected the doll in the water was her son, I didn't believe or comprehend the magnitude of what I was saying. His mom didn't understand what this eight-year-old was saying and immediately dismissed me. I figured she either didn't want to think about the possibility of her son being dead and trapped in the river or didn't want to take a kid's word for it. I left there, and for the first time, it hit me that Manny was that doll and that he was dead. I didn't return to their home over the next few days and tried not to focus on the situation.

Unbeknownst to me, that following Wednesday, a week after Manny's disappearance, his mom convinced the cops to finally check out the tip I had offered over the weekend. That afternoon, we learned police had recovered his body from the same river spot I had pointed out. Police said the rushing water had wiped away any skin-color tone Manny had, and his hands were in a fist because he appeared to have been fighting. But what was he fighting? The police in Belize didn't do much of an investigation and chalked up Manny's death as a simple drowning. But many questions remained. Why was his body in a defensive pose? And how did he end up in the water in the first place? I had my own questions, including: Did he kill himself? Did someone in our ultraconservative and super-homophobic culture know about our interaction and kidnap and murder him? I couldn't sleep for weeks, and I could never explain to my family the extent of the trauma I buried within me.

Manny's funeral was one of the saddest things I've ever experienced. I felt a potent mixture of guilt, sadness, and fear. In our culture, showing emotion, especially crying, even at funerals, is frowned upon. I could barely hold back the tears as his tiny white coffin entered the church at the end of our street, just steps away from the forestry trail that led to the riverbank where I found his body. I sat on the end of one of the pews in the front because I wanted to be as close to him as possible in these last moments, as there would not be an open coffin. After all, he had been in the water so long. As the coffin passed within inches of my face, with his mom and young brother pushing it from behind, I placed my hand over my eyes to hide the tears.

The coroner's report confirmed the police findings and ruled Manny's death an accidental drowning, but that explanation did not convince his family or me. His mom and brother moved from the neighborhood a few months later, fearing something more nefarious was at work. She didn't want to take any chances with her surviving son, and I never saw them again.

Coming to America

I have no idea where my ambition to seek success came from, especially as a poor kid who grew up in a mud house, but I'm sure it had to do with the confluence of Manny's mysterious death, the PTSD of my sexual abuse, and my desire to have a life that looked as different as possible from the one I was born into.

My other brothers all pursued blue-collar careers, but I followed the ambition gifted to me by my creator in pursuing my goals. I also manifested getting out of Belize as a fight-or-flight response to my uncertainties regarding my sexuality in a homophobic country and culture. Fortunately, my mother had a plan over a decade in the making. Before I was born, my mom saved her tiny weekly earnings and paid "coyotes" to illegally smuggle my oldest brother across the Mexico–U.S. border. My brother Alrick Jr. joined the military and sponsored the entire family, including my five other brothers and parents, for U.S. green cards.

Landing in New York City for the first time at eleven years old on a chillier-than-normal early June morning marked the start of a period of personal wonderment, growth, and attempts at assimilation into my perception of American culture. It all combined for a reasonably tough adjustment. Although I thought I was escaping poverty and personal problems in Belize, it would be decades of spanning more than a dozen locations before I realized my struggles had less to do with my physical location than with my psyche.

CHAPTER TWO

America

There are few things I can imagine as jarring to a child in their formative years as being uprooted and moving to a new country, with new schools, meeting new friends, adapting to various accents and dialects, and acclimating to a vastly different culture.

We lived in a tiny one-bedroom apartment in Brooklyn's Bedford-Stuyvesant neighborhood, where nightly gunshots drowned out the haunting squeaks from the numerous mice caught in the glue traps set up throughout the different rooms. Who knew an apartment could have such an endless supply of rodents? We divided our one bedroom into several rooms and utilized bunk beds. I slept in my mom's bed at night. The entire environment would have been challenging for anyone, but I found it particularly difficult as my comfort with my sexuality evolved.

The measures I took to assimilate ranged from the mundane to the macabre. I would press my nose together with the mindset I could make it a more Anglo muzzle. I got an unnecessary circumcision (ouch!) at age thirteen, so that my private parts resembled the others in the locker room. I applied skin-whitening creams each night to lose my dark Caribbean tone following an encounter on my first day in my new American school in which a student, possibly out of curiosity, wonderment, or sheer racial stupidity, tried to rub off my skin color with a napkin. I asked my English teacher to tutor me for about thirty minutes after school so I could improve my vocabulary and lose my accent.

My English teacher, Mrs. Rodriguez, a middle-aged woman who had immigrated from Nicaragua about a decade earlier, had this bit of sage advice on losing my thick Belizean accent and learning American grammar: "Listen to the music of The Carpenters," she encouraged me. "They sing slowly, softly, and with the simplest words from the dictionary," she said. "It's the purest American accent you will find." I wasn't sure what to make of this advice from a woman who sounded like she'd crossed the Rio Grande even after I did and was suspect that a duo from Southern California could teach me a Middle America dialect. But as an impressionable preteen, I soaked it in and embraced this concept as the key to my linguistic assimilation. Their smooth melodies, harmonic sounds, and simplistic lyrics were mesmerizing, and, over the course of five years, they helped me lose my Belizean accent and acquire a somewhat neutral one.

I learned the words to all their songs, but it would be years before I realized that in addition to helping with my assimilation to American culture, the music of The Carpenters was also providing the soundtrack to my sadness. From "Rainy Days and Mondays" to "Goodbye to Love" and "Now," with their dark lyrics of spurned love and unhappy days, I would play their songs on repeat during my darkest mental health moments.

In the eyes of a young immigrant landing in the United States in my most formative years, all that mattered was fitting into American society and culture and chasing my dream of having the sort of perceived fame, fortune, and happiness of everyone I saw on television as a kid just a few years prior in Belize. In keeping with an age-old Caribbean tradition, pirating, Belize received television for the very first time in 1981. I initially wanted to be a baseball player—Belize was obsessed with the Cubs because the Chicago television station WGN was the first station pirated—but during my tryout in high school, I was in outfield and went to catch a fly ball. It somehow evaded my glove and sliced my forehead, and my baseball stardom dreams were quickly deferred. I decided I would pursue a career in television instead.

My post-school routine in Brooklyn was pretty monotonous. I usually skipped any after-class activities and sat in front of our tiny thirteen-inch color television in the living room and watched the news. I was obsessed with the local anchors, including WABC's Roz Abrams, who had a television commercial that encouraged viewers to say hello to her on the street. (At every level of my broadcast career, I felt this would appear to be a terrible idea.) The ad was so convincing, I followed up and cold-called Roz, and much to my surprise, the switchboard operator connected me directly to her office. I asked her many questions about the business and inquired about internships; she couldn't have been friendlier and more supportive of this random kid who wanted to pursue a job in this field.

Standups and Letdowns

There were very few years between my arrival in the United States and college, so I spent little time researching where I would go for higher education. One day, in my high school guidance counselor's office, I saw a poster from the State University of New York at Oswego that featured a beautiful sunset over a massive body of water with a dormitory building in the background. I thought it was a stunning setting, and after learning they had a campus-run television station (a rarity at the time) and allowed unlimited internships, I was sold.

I had never visited Oswego before attending first-year orientation, and we didn't have Google to research or read the campus reviews. I had no idea that a beautiful, sunny, seemingly warm campus photo that was so inviting for me was probably taken in the *one* week when it is bright and warm in Oswego. Within a week of checking into the residence hall in early September, we had a freeze warning. By October, I experienced my first lake-effect blizzard, and the cold in November was beyond anything I had imagined. I felt hoodwinked. Oswego was located a six-hour drive from New York City on the banks of Lake Ontario and averaged about 112 inches of snow each winter, not to mention the additional pounding it received in the fall and spring.

Most people reflect on their college years and think about all the wild partying (if they could remember them). I reflect on how I wasted those fun years by being so driven to achieve early television success. I rarely went to bars or social events in my first few years of college. In hindsight, I was still relatively introverted and staving off any interaction that could turn sexual or romantic. I attended fraternity parties due to peer pressure and stood against the walls like a wet noodle, especially since I didn't drink (though I made up for that plenty later in life).

I recognized something was a bit off mentally. I initially didn't have suicidal thoughts, but I spent several nights of the week, especially in my senior year, crying myself to sleep. I tried to hit on girls, probably as part of my attempts at assimilation, but I think they knew, even if I didn't. When I finally got the nerve to ask a girl out on a date, she told me, "I have to do laundry." After three years in college, I was still a virgin.

I had cast aside childhood PTSD somewhere in my brain, but a prevailing feeling of fear and dread still guided me. That all got tested in the spring of my senior year. I had moved into a towering concrete block of residence halls that would make Soviet-era architects proud. As drab as the buildings were, they boasted spectacular unobstructed views of massive Lake Ontario, though for most of the year, this also meant watching the formation of the next lake-effect snowstorm.

The rooms were divided into suites and reserved for juniors, seniors, and those in the extended college plans. Everyone retreated to their pods, rarely mingling in the residence halls; you could go all year without seeing someone on the same floor, which I loved.

On the first day of senior year, I was moving into Onondaga Hall with two large boxes in tow when I noticed one of the welcoming committee members. His "Hello, welcome!" went from a friendly greeting to intense eye-to-eye contact to a look back. I may have been terrible at the gay game at this point in my life, but I knew enough that the "look back" meant it was on like *Donkey Kong*. He chased me down to the elevator bank to introduce himself. "Hi, I'm Thomas Cowder." I was left speechless by his brevity, especially in that collegiate era, and perhaps a little breathless, having carried two heavy boxes from the car to the elevator without much of a pause. I assumed he was straight because everyone seemed to be at that conservative state school. Through his nerdy round wire-rimmed glasses, I scoped his beautiful crystal-blue eyes, which were even more striking against his dark olive skin, and he had a lovely muscular frame.

Thomas had also lived in Onondaga the previous year and went to the same dining hall, yet this was our first time setting eyes on each other. The rush of emotions I felt that day was matched only by that initial thrill when Manny and I kissed about ten years prior. Thomas grabbed one of my boxes, rode up the elevator to the top floor with me, and showed me around my new suite. He knew the lay of the land, as he was the floor's resident assistant (RA). He then went over house rules, which ironically included no romantic interaction with the residence hall staff. It would turn out that the last part wasn't necessarily a decree.

For someone I hadn't seen once the previous year, Thomas and I ran into each other quite a bit after that first day, from the cafeteria to the gym and the hallway. Despite our nearly daily interactions, it would be several months before anything progressed.

In my senior year, I routinely drove an hour north of Oswego to tiny Watertown, New York, for my final internship as a student. It was the 178th largest television market in the country, and being so small and short-staffed, the station allowed its interns to report on-air. It was an invaluable opportunity for anyone starting their career, much less someone still in school. Most television stations are affiliated with one of the four big networks—ABC, NBC, CBS, and FOX—but the city of Watertown was so tiny and had so few viewers, channel 7 was the CBS, NBC, and FOX affiliate all rolled into one. They were able to cherry-pick programs from each of those networks on any given day.

When I arrived at WWNY in Watertown one autumn day for my internship, I felt like I had driven my car into some form of wintry abyss that had been frozen in time. The facility was located on the far end of the three-light downtown main street and was the size of a miniature old-school Blockbuster brick-and-mortar store. Soon after walking through the newsroom doors, the crew, while incredibly friendly, all made note that I was the first Black intern in the station's then forty-year history. The station's equipment seemed out of the TV Stone Age. The cameras were massive, with a separate tape recorder that doubled as a battery pack reminiscent of the bulky, cumbersome gear astronauts would don on spacewalks. The anchors were also producers, writers, graphic designers, and station management. The teleprompters, the devices that magically appear in front of the screens as we stare at the cameras but are not noticeable to viewers, were incredibly archaic. As an intern, one of my jobs was to apply Scotch tape from one piece of script paper to the other and roll it along on a motorized oval bed while a camera took a video of it and projected it as the anchors read.

I knew this place would be an opportunity for me to get my first on-air role, and one week after joining as an intern, it happened. One of the station's solo weekend reporters called out sick, and I showed up to the station and got called into the big leagues. It would be my first day on television. We decided to do a story on what was an emerging problem for the area's vibrant winter sport community: some radical people on something called a snowboard were impeding on the experience of traditional skiers. A photographer and I went to the local ski resort and talked with a bunch of pissed-off skiers and tried our best to speak with some snowboarders, but the sport was so new and unfamiliar even to them that few could get the hang of stopping for this TV crew at the base of the mountain.

Then came the moment I had been waiting for. During most television stories, there's something called a standup in which the reporter riffs for about ten or fifteen seconds, normally in the middle, saying something evergreen. This was about to be my television debut. I was on the precipice of what had become my obsession, especially since leaving Belize. I knew what I wanted to say, some random statistic about how many people consider themselves snowboarders versus skiers. I was given the countdown: three, two, one...

And I froze. I couldn't think of the statistic and couldn't think past my pounding heartbeat. I started to sweat in the twenty-degree cold. The photographer assured me it was okay and to try again. And after we counted down, I managed a few words before staring at that dark black glass hole of the camera and froze again.

Back at the station, the photographer walked to my desk to give me a count. I was embarrassed to learn it had taken us thirty-eight takes and the better half of an hour for me to get the standup right. Thankfully he was a veteran and good at his job, and the story turned out to be an amazing debut. I sat in the newsroom and watched my story on an old tube television fighting back tears, but this time with my heart pounding with pride. This was my start. I had no idea what that moment would lead to over the next few decades.

The Watertown internship was worth it for me to give up my college weekends for the chance of making a résumé reel by graduation day. One Saturday afternoon, as one of our legendary lake-effect storms was barreling down on us, the roads proved too dangerous to drive even for us hardened winter road warriors. I skipped my internship that weekend and stayed in the suite while everyone was at fraternity and sorority parties and the bars. Despite the approaching massive storm, Oswego students were conditioned to trekking through the worst of Mother Nature to take advantage of two Natural Light Beer deals.

That November Saturday evening was Thomas's designated night as the RA on duty, and after he made his rounds walking the building, he knocked on my suite door and invited me to come over to watch a movie. The main benefit of being a resident assistant in Onondaga was having an entire suite (which usually holds six people) to yourself. My suite was only three doors down from his, but that walk seemed like the most prolonged, most terrifying, most exulting fifty feet of my life. It was a mix of emotions: excitement, arousal, dread, and despair over the realization that something romantic was on the verge of happening.

Thomas popped on a movie as I sat on the far end of the living room couch. He offered me my first beer, which I thought would calm my nerves but didn't. He gave me pizza and dipped it in ranch dressing, which I had never had before and considered the whitest thing I'd ever put in my mouth to date. Slowly, throughout the movie, Thomas made his way closer to me on the couch, and with every inch, I got more nervous. My breath increasingly shortened, and those goose bumps expanded to full-on sweat bubbles on my skin. I wondered if he could tell how nervous I was. He reached over to hug me; it only made the nervous shaking I was experiencing even worse. "I'm really sorry," I told him, "I've never been with a dude before, or at least in this fashion." I lied, somewhat, as the pain from that last encounter with Manny remained ripe in my mind.

Tom reached over for a kiss, and I tried to shy away, but he was aggressive. I countered, adding my tongue to the mix. It was the weirdest experience—I kept thinking about Manny and my mom and how disappointed she would be in me for doing this. And as Thomas's tongue explored every corner of my mouth, the worst thing possible occurred: I imagined I was kissing Manny. I was no longer there with Thomas but had teleported to about a decade earlier. I could see Manny's face and eyes; I felt his soft, curly black hair at the tip of my fingers and smelled the citrus body soap on his skin. I was not in that moment with Tom. Once I returned to reality, I literally snapped, pulling back from his kiss with an unfortunate embarrassing guttural scream of "no."

Well, that was awkward.

Thomas grabbed me, held me in his arms, and attempted to reassure me. "It's okay," he said. "It happens." It was too late; this was already such an embarrassing episode. The tears began to flow uncontrollably. All of this was after just a simple kiss. My brain flashed through a series of emotions and introspections: what my Christian mom would think...the image of Manny's pale white arm above the surface of that river, just days after we'd kissed. There were also small flashbacks to my early childhood abuse.

I was a wreck. I lay there shaking for several more minutes, the tears flowing, my heart pounding, and little more than childlike whimpers emerging from my mouth. After my emotions subsided slightly, I once again apologized to Thomas and slowly got up to leave. Frayed nerves replaced my earlier excitement when I'd walked toward his suite, and my head was firmly sunken. It was a completely different walk of shame.

The next day, I saw Thomas walking through the cafeteria. Even though it was hard to miss each other, I pretended I didn't see him. A friend even snickered as we walked past him about Thomas being a fag. That word sent a jolt through me at the realization that I, too, based on my actions last night, was probably seen as a fag by others.

Despite living just yards away from each other, I never spoke with Thomas again. My PTSD was in full force, as I expected to see Thomas's lifeless body washing up on the shores of Lake Ontario any day. Since Manny, it was my singular prevailing thought whenever I entertained romantic encounters.

Dreams and Despair

I suffered one of my darkest mental health spirals following this experience. The same beautiful cliffs and sunsets that initially attracted me to Oswego on that poster in my high school guidance counselor's office now acted like a homing beacon toward death. I had been grappling with things since the weekend with Thomas and decided to head to an area just a few miles north of the campus called Sunset Bluffs, which boasted 150-foot-high cliffs overlooking the lake. In my early campus days, this was a place for stress relief and a space to reflect on life, especially at sunset. On this day, it was a place to contemplate what it would be like to die. It was the first time I'd flirted with and even enjoyed the thought of what it would be like to kill myself. I blasted Enya on my Walkman, entranced by the hypnotic synth sounds of "Sail Away" and the lyrics that summon you to leave it all behind. As the sun dipped beneath the horizon, I stared and was suddenly engulfed in tears. I walked to my car with my head down low, disappointed I couldn't complete the mission to end my life. It was, after all, a new ideation, and I was only eighteen years old. As distraught and depressed as I felt,

I couldn't bring myself to jump off that cliff. It was the first time I realized I needed help.

In Belize, anyone with mental health issues was just classified as crazy, even if it resulted from PTSD. I never addressed my issues after the sexual abuse and trauma from Manny's death because I didn't want to consider myself insane, a stigma that prevented me from getting help. I was surrounded by people who, if they knew, would have been more than supportive, but I felt mentally marooned. I never disclosed to anyone the battle I was fighting. Outwardly, I was a fun, happy college student with much to live for. Despite the internal struggles, that exterior shell would become a hallmark for the next two decades.

I walked to the doctor's office the next day, hoping they'd give me pills to help lift my mood. I saw the campus general practitioner. "I'm not here for anything physical," I informed him. "I just need something not to make me want to ki—" I broke down in tears at the realization that I was suicidal. I felt like an alcoholic at his first AA meeting, and that initial declaration of the problem was difficult. The doctor removed his latex gloves and cradled my head in his chest while I cried uncontrollably. He whispered in my ear that he wasn't qualified to treat me and went to the in-house psychiatrist next door.

She immediately made room for me to sit down with her. "Would you like to talk about what you're going through?" I responded negatively by shaking my head. *What am I doing here?* I thought, with no intention of admitting my childhood trauma or grappling with my sexuality. With a soft voice, the psychiatrist reached over and reassuringly muttered, "It's okay. I'll be here whenever you're ready." She made an appointment for me to see her the next day. I woke up the next morning, called the office, postponed it for the following day, and never showed up for that appointment.

That was the beginning of my need-slash-hate relationship with the therapy field. I spent the next two decades going to head doctors when I had nowhere else to turn, but I rarely followed up after my initial visits. "Go to therapy" or "you need therapy" was often beaten into my brain whenever people learned of my depression. I've had therapists to the stars, seen gay and bi ones, sat on couches of doctors of different races and ethnicities—and I lied my way through each of those experiences.

"I just broke up with my girlfriend, and it's making me depressed."

"I'm suffering PTSD from all the death and destruction I've witnessed with my job."

"My dog died, and I can't recover."

At no point did I come close to addressing the real problems, mainly because I wasn't confident about the genesis of my depression. Was it the childhood abuse? Fear and self-loathing about being bisexual at a time when it wasn't widely tolerated or even talked about? Or was it the stress of succeeding and not returning to the poverty that dominated most of my early life?

After college, I studied the anchoring styles of newscasters I liked, including Bryant Gumbel and Katie Couric. Bryant had an off-camera side glance that I found intriguing—who or what was he looking at in that moment?—and Katie used her reputation as "America's Sweetheart" to disarm her interview subjects, as she did during a fluff White House tour when she turned the tables on an unsuspecting President George Bush Sr. and suddenly grilled him on the Iran–Contra scandal. I liked that approach of smiling while you land a killer question.

I did everything to set myself up for a successful broadcast career, including growing my Jheri curl, exploiting my ambiguously gendered name, and dressing in drag in some of my mom's clothes. I landed my first internship at *The Today Show* because I was told the network morning shows only wanted female interns. I was initially turned down for a *Good Morning America* internship with Joan Lunden's office because I wasn't female. I learned from that interview, and this time my *Tootsie* ploy worked. When I showed up several months later for my first day of the internship, sans female clothing and my Jheri curl gone, my supervisors had fortunately forgotten what I looked like.

My tenure at *Today* was invaluable. I sat in on production meetings with then executive producer Jeff Zucker, lunched with Couric, got one-on-one advice from Jane Pauley, and watched firsthand that Gumbel off-camera glance (it turns out he wasn't looking at anything in particular). I soaked up as much advice as anyone was willing to dispense. I followed it with another five summer and mid-semester internships at nationwide television outlets. It paid off; I landed my first reporting job shortly after leaving college at an NBC station in Rochester, New York—considered a medium-size television market. But I was so new to the business that a photographer told me, "You're so green that if I didn't know better, I'd say you were Irish." I was green, all right—it would be years before I got the punchline of that joke.

Being on-air in Rochester was everything I had imagined. I was one of the few Black guys on television in a small town, and as such, I was locally famous. I was already living my broadcast dream, and I spent three years in Rochester before reluctantly departing for FOX Philadelphia in what was supposed to have been a massive career move. Overnight, I went from the seventy-sixth largest television market in the country to the fourth largest market (ironically, the station was located at the corner of Fourth and Market Streets).

It was in Philadelphia where I realized for the first time since my college experience that I was suffering from mental health issues. I became aware of my depression and anxiety manifesting itself in minor panic attacks. Though they are different conditions, they're often a one-two punch when you're mired in mental health misery.

I was in a big market though barely making minimum wage, paying an agent 10 percent of my salary, figuring out my sexuality, living in a city at the time I couldn't quite connect with (a place I regarded as a glorified gas station between Washington and New York), and working obscenely early morning hours. I've since come to appreciate and respect Philadelphia and its residents deeply, but in the late '90s, all those factors contributed to my mental deterioration and my frequent suicidal ideation. I tried over-the-counter homeopathic drugs (St. John's wort) and would spend most of my nonwork hours at home, sleeping and crying while listening to The Carpenters. Not surprisingly, I left Philadelphia early in my contract and returned home to New York. My struggles with depression were only beginning.

Burnout and Broadcasting

The carpet inside the elevators at 30 Rockefeller Plaza, where NBC is headquartered, is covered with the famed peacock logo. On my first day as a cub reporter, I found it fitting (and nerdy) to look down at that trademark while listening to the John Williams's "Mission Theme," the *NBC Nightly News* anthem. I had used my connections through the National Association of Broadcasters to land a freelance role as a New York–based NBC News correspondent. It had been ten years since I entered the building as an intern, and now, as an official correspondent, it felt like I had arrived. The job, however, was a grind that required being available 24/7, always dependent on the will of the news gods. Then came the attacks on September 11.

I lived on Seventh Avenue in Manhattan just a few miles from the Twin Towers. The night and early morning prior, I had been hosting two friends from the UK, and we had partied hard. Shortly after 8:46 a.m., the first plane struck the North Tower, and an endless series of fire trucks could be heard from my place blaring their sirens as they drove down to Lower Manhattan. In hindsight, I realize that for many of those firefighters I saw buzzing past me that morning, it was the last few moments of their lives.

With an epic hangover, I dressed and went down to the World Trade Center to meet my producer and crew, who were on the way. First, by subway (I made it one stop before all train service was canceled), then by taxi (I made it one block before sitting in traffic for half an hour), and finally by running and walking. September 11, 2001, was a beautiful but warm day, especially if you were lugging a massive bag carrying a cumbersome old-school laptop and various audio and video equipment to be able to plug in and get on the air. I made it as close as I could get to Ground Zero, within ten city blocks, when the South Tower collapsed.

My brain couldn't grasp the magnitude of what I was watching half a mile away, so I stood there frozen while crowds ran away from the ever-growing debris cloud. Finally, I snapped out of it, joined in the hurried escape from Lower Manhattan, and headed toward 30 Rockefeller Plaza. I got about halfway back to the headquarters on Sixth Avenue when I noticed the crowd in front of me had stopped and was looking back toward the Twin Towers. I looked around to observe a massive dust cloud where both towers had stood. "The second tower fell," some random stranger told me. I tried calling the office on my cell phone to get instructions on where to go, but all the lines were down, so I continued toward 30 Rock. There were so many rampant rumors, including one that the NBC HQ would be a target for terrorists next, but despite a few extra layers of security, I made it to the office.

The next few weeks were a blur. As journalists, we pride ourselves on being able to distance ourselves from the emotional weight of the stories we cover. This was the first story to really impact my already fragile mental health state. Working as a journalist in New York in those days meant living and breathing the story, but the anxiety surrounding 9/11 was on another spectrum. I would work twelve-hour shifts as a correspondent, be surrounded by armed National Guard soldiers on street corners once I got home, and could smell the burning building debris once I left the house to grab dinner.

It was like that for weeks, which drove me to my second attempt at therapy. A friend recommended an Upper West Side therapist who was popular with plenty of celebrities. After several weekly sessions, in which I would cry about my stress level and rip my emotions wide open only for my time to be up until the following week, I finally had a breakthrough. I needed to escape the environment and hard news track I was on because it contributed to my overall mental health decline.

I set out on a new career path that seemed nearly impossible at the outset because the post-9/11 television industry had suddenly shifted its focus almost exclusively toward hard news and away from entertainment reporting and fluffy content—which was precisely the sort of work I wanted to pursue as a solution for my sanity. The only stories I would pitch to my producers were entertainment- or lifestyle-related. In my post-9/11 days, I built up my résumé tape with entertainment material to position me for that next role—less death and destruction, and more glitz and glamour.

I volunteered to report for the local NBC station on Friday mornings to preview *The Today Show*'s summer concert artists as they rehearsed in the 6:00–7:00 a.m. hour in the dark at Rockefeller Center. I pushed to do the red carpet at the Rockefeller Center Christmas Tree Lighting, where I met tons of celebrities, including a then-eleven-year-old who, with her momager (mom manager) acting as a publicist, would crash significant events in hopes that unsuspecting reporters would interview her and give free publicity to a completely unknown artist. I distinctly recall passing on the opportunity to interview a young Taylor Swift during one of those red carpet crashes.

My missed shot at being an early discoverer of Taylor Swift notwithstanding, my quick career-shift plan worked. I soon landed an entertainment anchor role at CNN in Atlanta. I was about to escape the daily grind of hard news, but my mental health decline would only intensify to epic and very public proportions.

CHAPTER 3

Trip One: Hawaii + MDMA + Arizona = Forgiveness

There are few places you'll find with more contrasting experiences than on Maui's southwest coast, where Makena's Big Beach sits. Its expansive geography lends to the descriptive name—the beach is a mile and a half long and more than thirty yards wide, which is big for most beaches. The sand is soft and supple, a blinding beige in the midday sun. The water on any given day, an array of beautiful blues and greens, is often rough, with waves not recommended for beginner swimmers. Still, this spectacular beach just four miles south of the island's most popular resorts in Wailea draws vacationing families from all over the world. Yet, the wholesome family fun at Big Beach contrasts starkly with the clothing-optional activities taking place just a few yards away on Little Beach, which is separated by a tiny volcanic bluff slicing into the ocean, no taller than fifteen feet high or wider than ten feet.

I visited those beaches one day in May in the early 2000s with a group of friends to celebrate a fortieth birthday. I had been doing morning television at CNN for more than a year, and my depression had reached a borderline clinical level. My friends figured if the sun, surf, and sexy luau dancers couldn't lift this cloud of depression, nothing could, and it didn't—at least initially. We made road trips to the red, black, and multicolored beaches and took the bait to drive to Hana, only to realize an important life lesson: the journey is the reward. After nearly three hours of moving up the road's winding path to Hana, I faced the disappointment that the highlight was a small high school and an overpriced resort.

Despite being in paradise, very little brought me joy. At this point, I had spent decades hiding and running from the tremendous traumas of my childhood and from my bisexuality. I placed it in a mental lockbox, but one that felt as if it was eroding with time, its darkness seeping slowly out into my veins. I had not experienced love or had an actual sexual relationship, and I was in my late twenties. I had cut myself off, and the emotions were boiling to eruption levels rivaling Kilauea.

Our group took the four-mile drive south of our hotel to explore Big Beach on Sunday afternoon. Makena was one of the most impressive beaches I've ever visited. The sand was blinding with the solar reflection but so soft. We relaxed for hours on our blankets, sunbathing more than swimming because the water was too rough. We kept noticing people walking on top of a jetty at one end of the beach and disappearing. Were they entering a flat earth abyss?

I was curious and walked over to check it out. Over the years, the locals had carved a path within this volcanic jetty so that as soon as you walk into the trail, the towering rocks obscure your vision from the rest of the Makena beach crowd. After a couple of turns and elevation changes, you descend into...well, debauchery. There were naked bodies everywhere. People were dancing in the nude, sunbathing naked, standing around naked, and nude bodysurfing. (Whoever knew that was a thing?) If Woodstock were a beach festival, this was it. In my head, the Fifth Dimension provided the soundtrack for all I saw. It was the Age of Aquarius and every freaky astrological sign there could be. People were naked while making out, dancing, smoking, and bodysurfing, and beyond the tree line, I'd later learn that people were communing with each other. I ran back through the jetty to tell my friends. I had never been to a nude beach and had no interest in seeing the other members of my group naked, but I figured it would make for a great story with the crew. We made the short hike to Little Beach, leaving the familial paradise for this unknown underworld. Our group of three men and two women, none of whom were in a relationship with each other, was now faced with a big dilemma: Do we drop trou?

We walked past several different body types as we went behind the trees to get naked. (I am not sure why we removed our clothes in private when we'd soon be naked for all the beach to see.) I have anchored newscasts with no teleprompter, scripts, or reporters to toss to and no direction from my control room. Yet, I've never felt as physically and mentally naked as I was then. I ran, not walked, from the trees straight into the Pacific Ocean. Fortunately for me, Little Beach is a fraction of the size of its neighbor, Makena, which left little exposure to the elements.

On the other hand, my friends slowly made their way to the ocean, not an ounce of timidity in their blood. I had one of the better bodies on the beach, thanks to my depression diet and obsession with my undiagnosed body dysmorphic disorder. However, I associated nudity with sexuality and wasn't comfortable with either topic. As I stood in the ocean, skinny-dipping for the first time, I looked back at the beach and was envious of all those others frolicking comfortably in the buff. I had never been in a sex-positive environment like this before; I had spent decades suppressing my sexuality and avoiding sexual contact with anyone.

A Little Beach Sunday tradition began as the sun dropped to the west. Unlike most beaches, the population grew as the sun set. Soon, a circle formed in the sand as people traded portable speakers, blasting different music genres. Several drummers gathered within that circle as the crowd surrounded them, many dancing, mostly nude. (I quickly learned that certain dance moves should not be performed in the buff.) I had made my way in from the ocean and sat on the beach with my cell phone covering my bits, cultural myth be damned. Suddenly, I felt this flash of heat rush past the top of my head. I looked back, surprised to see two guys literally playing with fire in the nude. They shot flames from their mouths as they moved from the back of the crowd, where a path had been cleared for them as they moved closer to the drums. They proceeded to twirl and spin their batons in a mesmerizing dance-off. My crew edged closer to the circle in full Woodstock hippie-dancing mode. *They have to be on something*, I thought to myself. Still, it was a mostly friendly, life-embracing experience. The drum circle got tighter as people gathered closer to watch the spinning fire in the foreground of the ever-changing sunset hue over the Pacific Ocean.

We gravitated toward a group of tourists from Wisconsin who were also there for a birthday celebration. I locked eyes with one of the most beautiful men I've ever met. He was a tall, handsome blue-eyed blond straight out of a Scandinavian *Vogue* magazine. The colonial culture of Belize had indoctrinated me to believe that White, blond, and blue-eyed were among the elements that epitomized beauty. That thinking was entrenched from childhood; my mom even saw Princess Margaret during one of her royal visits to Belize. The old belief was, "If you see a pretty lady while pregnant, you'll have a beautiful daughter." My mom was pregnant with my brother Al and had neither a daughter nor a good-looking child. It would take many years for me to deprogram myself from that bias.

"Hi, I'm Tyler," he said to me. He was about twenty-one to my thirty years of age, and he couldn't have been more central casting, Midwest edition, if he had tried.

From smiling to squinting his eyes and stroking his thick blond curly hair, his every move appeared in slow motion to me. His soft gaze seemed to pierce my soul, baring it raw for the world to see, only to massage it and return it warmly into my body. I had no idea what had gotten into me. The expanding group of drummers and fire dancers encircled us, but we didn't notice; no one and nothing else mattered except for the two of us at that moment. I even forgot that I was buck-ass naked; I was so into his personality and aura I didn't even look down to check out his goods.

Tyler and I retreated to the darkness beyond the tree line, putting our clothes back on (which seems odd after meeting someone and being sexually attracted to them) and spending more than an hour wavering between talking about our lives and kissing. The romance butterflies were back for the first time in over a decade, and I wasn't even drunk or high on anything. Yes, I had gone on dates since college, and I had seen the potential of a possible relationship with a number of people, though I always hesitated to take it further. But this was different—an impulsive, organic meeting of two kindred souls. Still, as my feelings started to flow throughout my body from this encounter, a deep-seated dread began to take hold of me, and butterflies quickly gave way to a pit in my stomach. As much as I was there, in the moment, kissing this beautiful person, I was also mentally transported back to my past. My brother. Manny. The college dorm room.

And then Tyler, the kid from Wisconsin, barely out of his teens, suggested we take a tab of Molly. At that point, I had only a casual knowledge of the drug. Many of my New York City friends would take one or two pills to get them through a regular weekend at the famous gay club, Splash, and by Tuesday, they could not leave the house, much less function because of the serotonin drain that takes place. It just didn't sound like a good idea to someone already grappling with depression. "This is not the same as X," he said, attempting to reassure me. "It's a more pure form of the drug. There'll be less of a Tuesday hangover."

I wasn't sure I was buying what this Midwest marketing student was selling me. I had heard so many horror stories of people dying by suicide in the days after a wild ecstasy bender. But if it had a calming, numbing effect like the weed did at dinner earlier in the trip, maybe it was worth doing to help with my childhood PTSD. "It'll also make this here so much more exhilarating," he said. I was so attracted to Tyler, but the last thing I wanted to do was transform into a blubbering embarrassment on the beach. "Whatever is causing you to tremble right now, trust me, Molly will make it a whole lot better."

I'm not sure how much I believed what he was saying, but I surrendered to it anyway because I wanted to live in the moment without the childhood trauma. He unwrapped a small piece of aluminum foil, and inside were four or five capsules. He told me he placed them in these gelatin cases so that he could travel with them, and TSA would easily mistake them for supplements or vitamins. I grabbed one of the pills, swallowed it with a beer chaser, and suddenly Tyler's lips were pressed against mine. What followed was an all-consuming make-out session on the forest floor. I was so into the moment and music I forgot that it had been hours since I'd seen my friends. Just as the combination of flutters and fears strangled my heart, something else kicked in: the ecstasy.

"The lights!" I screamed out suddenly and randomly.

"Yeah, we're looking at the same lights that we've been staring at for the last twenty minutes; you're on your comeuppance," Tyler said, referring to my Molly high kicking into effect. "Welcome," he said laughingly. It felt like being on one of the world's fastest roller coasters, shooting me 140 miles an hour in less than five seconds, with no idea of how or when I would get down once at the top of the ride. In the middle of the comeuppance, as I was dancing and smiling uncontrollably, Tyler grabbed both my arms to try to take hold of my flailing and stared into my eyes. I was entirely into my Woodstock 1960s dance moves, I imagined. Tyler stopped moving and I tried staring into his eyes, but it was like doing an eye exam while driving at high speed.

Despite an overwhelming sensation of vertigo, I was cognizant of everything and everyone and loved life. Unbeknownst to my mind, my face had developed an unrelenting ear-to-ear smile. As Tyler grabbed my arms and looked at me lovingly, gone were the trepidations; the only thing I felt was unmitigated excitement. I loved this moment and this life. *What was this crazy drug to make me feel this way?!* Even my PTSD mind couldn't ruin this feeling for me. Tyler expanded the embrace of my arms to a full-on hug and then reached in again to kiss me. This was on another level; I felt it tingle through my body. I was so happy being touched, kissed, and cared for. I thought of the lingering dread following Manny's death, the sexual abuse by my relative, and even my encounter with Thomas in college, but my brain had rested those traumas in a lockbox. I didn't know what to make of it; I knew I didn't want it to end. We danced together, touched every part of each other's bodies, and kissed seemingly endlessly; I had never been happier. I wondered, *Was this all because of the ecstasy or something unique to Tyler?* I had no idea, but I knew it was a substance seemingly altering everything I'd come to associate with any form of sexual interaction. I was turned on, my heartbeat rhythms synced with the fire dance. I was dancing with Tyler, holding his hands, smiling from ear to ear, and fantasizing about being with him in every aspect.

We stood (sitting and remaining motionless was not an option on this drug) holding hands, watching the symphonies of bodies silhouetted by dusk. I felt love, joy, euphoria, and just plain old tingles. *This drug is wondrous*, I thought. We reached over to each other and gently kissed while soaking in the music, moment, and Molly, only to be interrupted by my friends whom I had long abandoned for this stranger from the Midwest. I could barely restrain my childish, impish giddiness or excitement about anything and everything. I rattled off a quick dissertation of emotion-peppered observations.

"Isn't this the most fantastic place ever?"

"I've never been this happy in my entire life."

"That fire dance is the most beautiful thing I've ever experienced. Is this what it's like to give birth to a child?"

"I'm in love."

That last part garnered a "you're fucking high" response from my friend Rick. He and I had met a few years earlier while working together at CNN and struck up a close friendship. We were in Hawaii celebrating his fortieth birthday, and as such, Rick felt the added pressure of ensuring everyone was having a great time. What I didn't realize was that while I was in the ocean earlier, he inquired about and then encouraged Tyler to ply me with Molly. He looked on with a satisfied grin as Tyler and I kept rubbing our hands on each other due to the drug's propensity to enhance affectionate touches.

"I love you so much, I can't imagine being anywhere else with anyone else," I said. Rick noted this was a complete reversal from my demeanor just twelve hours earlier. My body could no longer contain the energy flowing through my veins; I needed to move. I removed the remaining articles of clothing I was wearing and encouraged Tyler to do the same. I grabbed his hand, ran past the flurry of revelers dancing and hypnotized by the light show on the sand, and leaped into the Pacific. Unlike my earlier dash to the water, this time I felt free, proud, and uninhibited. I had never contemplated the molecular makeup of water before that very moment, and as my body interacted with the ocean, I felt every element rolling across my skin.

Tyler and I danced in waist-deep water to the drums. The reflection of the swirling flames bounced a mesmerizing glow against the waves. It was euphoria on overload. We remained there for what seemed like hours, kissing, touching, and embracing, soaking in the sounds, sights, and sensations, but when we returned to the beach, our friends said we had only been in the sea for ten minutes. The space-time continuum is on another level when you're rolling on Molly—probably the reason people attending raves feel the need to re-up and get another quick hit, under the misguided belief that they had been partying on the drug for a long time. For us, the drug had been in our system for only about an hour, so we joined the dance circle around the blindingly bright lights of the fire and capitulated to the beats and rhythms. Our bodies moved in a wobbly wavelike motion, an unrelenting smile on my face, my heart full and incessantly pounding. I was happy. I felt love, and I had no fear.

When you start feeling the effects of Molly, it's similar to those first thirty seconds on a roller coaster ride as you're strapped in and are raised to the ride's peak point. And then, at the top of the ride, the medicine's g-forces go into overdrive, with your body feeling the weight of the onset of the drug before it takes your mind on a mesmerizing ride through loops and curves. And similar to a coaster, as you begin your "come down" from Molly, there's a recognition of what an exhilarating experience it had been, mixed with some sadness that it's over. It's around this time that many will do another dose, but not me—I was satiated. I looked over at Tyler and simply said, "Thank you." I felt like he had changed my life, because this drug had allowed me to have my first positive sexual experience. I kissed him again, hugged him, said goodbye, and returned to my friends sitting in the sand, waiting for my roll to be done. They were more into weed, and some had taken mushrooms and long sobered up from their adventure; it was time to return to the hotel and pack up to depart for home the next day. That ear-to-ear smile finally eased early the next morning as I surrendered to sleep, my heart still full of love.

I knew I had changed somehow, but was it only a temporary bandage? Or was it a legitimate rewiring of my childhood and adolescent PTSD brain? It was still unclear. I wanted to know more.

The Power of MDMA Therapy

Despite my positive experience with MDMA, I was not interested in the form of recreational parties and sexualized usage commonly associated with it. I was, however, intrigued by its potential medicinal use for people like me. But in the early 2000s, very few spoke about any form of plant medicine for therapeutic use, much less studied it. Ecstasy, at one point, was commonly used in the United States and Europe for couples therapy and the treatment of trauma. That ended in 1985 when the Drug Enforcement Administration (DEA) made it a Schedule 1 drug, similar to heroin, LSD, and, strangely, marijuana as the highest category of controlled illegal substances.

The psychedelics renaissance for mental health treatment had been ushered in partly due to the work of MAPS, the Multidisciplinary Association for Psychedelic Studies, founded by Rick Doblin in 1986, on the heels of the DEA's new classification of psychedelics as being highly addictive drugs. Doblin has been a longtime drug activist, and through his nonprofit with MAPS and its sister company, the MAPS Public Benefit Corporation, he has pushed for the legalization of psychedelics as a form of therapy once again. Doblin told the *New York Times*, "The big tragedy to point out is that it was pretty clear, in the late 1970s and early 1980s, that MDMA had incredible therapeutic potential." He said, "All the suffering since then because MDMA was criminalized is enormous." Since 2001,

MAPS has devoted more than $12 million in research to legalize ecstasy-assisted treatment for PTSD, which affects an estimated 3.5 percent of the American population.

I was fascinated by the study, which spent years going through the rigorous Food and Drug Administration approval phases. Then, in 2022, a former CNN colleague who was familiar with one of the doctors leading the MAPS study encouraged me to get in touch with him. Once in contact with Dr. Joseph McCowan, I flew cross-country to the California Center for Psychedelic Therapy in Los Angeles to see him, but he was too tied up. We tried meeting on Zoom, but the scheduling didn't work out. Finally, we agreed to meet in Atlanta, where he hosted a Black psychedelics gathering.

McCowan is a rock star in this space, and getting to spend time with him was worth the trouble. He is a clinical psychologist and psychotherapist and one of the leading therapists in Phase 3 of the MDMA-assisted therapy for PTSD. As a biracial man, Dr. McCowan is passionate about spreading awareness and education about the healing benefits of psychedelics for people of color. He would be the perfect person to explain what was happening in my head when I took ecstasy and how it could have helped me confront my PTSD with positive results.

Dr. Joseph McCowan is a licensed doctor in several mental health fields, with degrees from multiple universities and many awards, an accredited keynote speaker, and an internationally recognized expert on most things psychedelics. But as I sat five feet across from him in a suburban Atlanta Airbnb, I couldn't help but think how insanely sexy he was. Joseph, as he insisted I call him, sat on the other end of a couch, light-skinned Black, with a salt-and-pepper beard, perfectly sculpted bald head, and dimples deeper than the Los Angeles River. His style was very much the epitome of a Berkeley, California, mannequin, with a casual bohemian look from head to toe. His earth-toned jacket matched his skin-tight earthy pants, shin-high brown leather boots, and mildly acidic printed complimentary button-down shirt.

How can I progress in learning about anything scientific if he continues to look like this? I thought as he smirked at me with complete knowledge of my flirtation. Even if I attempted to reduce him to a pretty face, Joseph surpassed that. He'd spent several years as a co-therapist in the most critical research using MDMA-assisted treatment for PTSD, something that has the potential to revolutionize how doctors treat patients suffering from everything from childhood abuse to postwar mental trauma. "We're at a pivotal point in history," he said as he described the current movement to legalize psychedelics for treatment. MDMA will soon revolutionize how doctors all across the United States will treat patients with various levels of trauma. "Think of therapy," he told me, "like a greenhouse, a safe place running the conditions for growth, a trusted place. But we, as therapists, can make the plants grow only so much. MDMA acts like a fertilizer that blossoms various plants of compassion, love, and serenity; those are the flowers of the process." It was a fascinating take, but I was curious: What was it about methylenedioxymethamphetamine that had this immense effect?

It is an empathogenic drug developed in 1912 by Merck—yeah, the same health company that gives us vaccines and prescription medicines. "The chemicals in the drug produce empathy-producing effects," Joseph said. "It can break the cycle of trauma that takes place in PTSD patients." He had a more scientific explanation that included the amygdala portion of the brain and how the drug worked to attach to the hippocampus. He went on with his big words. "MD causes the release of neurotransmitters, like dopamine, serotonin, norepinephrine, and oxytocin, into the brain cells. PTSD is the body and mind's way of distancing itself from that which is potentially retraumatizing." However it manifests itself, PTSD is, in actuality, a cognitive and physical defense mechanism. "The chemicals in the drug work as interceptors in the brain that help relax the built-up defenses and soften the stress," he said. As for why MDMA is suggested and not mushrooms, Dr. McCowan says it just so happens that the research is further along on MD, and it is yet to be determined whether psilocybin (the active ingredient in magic mushrooms) would be as effective in treating trauma.

Dr. McCowan summarized the therapy that got us to this point. Phase 1 ran from 2008 through 2010 and didn't involve any human participants. "The focus," he said, "was more to just look at the safety of MDMA." Following those initial results, researchers moved forward, combining the drug with talk therapy, which took place in Phase 2 in a controlled environment from 2012 through 2016 and featured more than 200 carefully screened participants worldwide. Dr. McCowan was a co-therapist in the Phase 3 final trials. They included a smaller group of 104 patients who suffered moderate to severe PTSD. Roughly half the team was given MDMA over eight-hour sessions, including talk therapy with a pair of doctors. Dr. McCowan and his colleagues had no idea which patients were given the placebo or MDMA.

The treatments were performed over four years from 2018 to 2022. The trials, he said, were part rave, with some participants breaking out in solo dance parties, part funeral, with others burying their trauma, and a bit of spiritual revival for those who had "come to Jesus" moments with their PTSD. "The patients developed a new relationship with their fear, and I strongly feel that anything you develop a new relationship with, you can feel safer."

The eight-hour time frame for each session allowed the drug to run its course through their minds and bodies entirely. The first dosage most patients received was about 125 milligrams by mouth, which usually took forty-five minutes for the "come up" to kick in. Two hours later, the doctors typically administered another half dosage. The clinical trial results, he said, were truly monumental.

"Nearly 90 percent of the group with MD saw a depletion in their symptoms, and 71 percent were so improved they were no longer considered clinically suffering PTSD. Compare that to 69 and 48 percent in the non-MDMA group. Without the support of MDMA, it was challenging for a person to be present with their traumatic material. Talking and exploring it internally for the eight-hour session with MDMA helped support the relationship with the therapist, with self, and with the trauma."

Joseph was not surprised by my perceived partial breakthrough from Molly in Maui. "It was the drug disarming you," he told me. I wondered how important the talk therapy aspect was to the success of MDMA as a treatment for my issues. "It's not necessary to undergo therapy before receiving the drug," he replied. "It is helpful, however, to have a road guide there as you enter different territory." I found this equal parts intriguing and intimidating—I wanted to pursue this journey through ecstasy but was very resistant to doing talk therapy because of my previous frustrations with it.

And then suddenly, it hit me. As I sat there on the other end of a comfortable brown L-shaped leather sofa, barely six feet from Joseph, and had spent now an hour speaking about my feelings and asking questions and getting plenty of time answering his, he had successfully Jedi mind-tricked me into my first ever successful talk therapy session. The revelation made me slightly open to a form of therapy involving MDMA. However, I was still reluctant to reveal my feelings to a medical professional, even if it involved Molly.

The Longest One-Night Stand

Perhaps it was a result of this journey, or the technological prowess of gay dating apps, or just because George P. Brown III is quite the looker, but in the fall of 2011, I met George while I was working as an anchor and reporter for WJLA, the local ABC affiliate in Washington, DC. It had been more than a decade since my experience in

Hawaii that allowed me to face the trauma of my abusive childhood and Manny's death and have a positive encounter. I was far from healed, but I'd spent years since Hawaii on dates with various men, and some women. I never wanted or thought I was capable of getting into a relationship, and that's why I felt at home being on the casual dating sites.

I met George on an app, and it was expected to be just a fling, but it has turned out to be the longest one-night stand of my life. He was as wholesome and stereotypically purebred as they come: a White boy from a cattle farm near Buffalo, New York, with looks out of a JCPenney catalog. He had that combination of crystal-blue eyes, dark hair, and megawatt smile that would make Lois Lane swoon. Following our first "encounter," I experienced the good butterflies that echoed the sensations felt in Hawaii. He had only recently emerged from the closet a few months earlier, and I was entrenched in my single existence. My aversion to a relationship or loving a significant other at this point in my life wasn't due to deep-seated fear but rather a lack of capability. Yet somehow, we connected, fell in love, and moved from Washington, DC, to New York together. The traumatizing thoughts about my relative and Manny were still there, but they were not debilitating to me or my relationship with George. But I also knew there was still some healing that was necessary. I just didn't know when, where, or how it would manifest.

Phoenix

3223 West Potter Drive in North Phoenix is about as unlikely a location for a rave or circuit party as one could imagine. Still, inside this obscure suburban home, I'd again experience MDMA. It was a relatively cool July evening in Phoenix (average high temperatures had finally dipped below 111 degrees) as I walked into this old ranch-style home, just a few blocks from the main east-west highway, for what would be an entirely different, equally impactful, but more enduring medicinal effect of using MDMA.

Just a week earlier, while in Phoenix for a birthday party, I had come across this beautiful woman in her mid-forties with long, straight brown hair that fell halfway down her back. Her soul connected with mine barely seconds after saying hello to each other. If Mattel had a desert hippie Barbie line, it would be Katya, a Polish-born mother of two who, like me, had moved to the United States at the age of eleven. In those first few minutes of interaction and afterward, our conversation spanned the gamut, from psychedelics (she recently became a medicine woman and conducted all forms of journeys) to the perils of moving to a new country at a young age (assimilating was an everyday struggle) to the power of the mind over our bodies (she lost two teeth in the past year and was convinced she would be able to regrow them by using her mind). I found her equal parts fascinating, empathetic, and somewhat quirky.

For context: Katya had also recently purchased thirty-eight acres of land near Flagstaff after receiving a "message" during a journey informing her that she needed to prepare a massive piece of real estate as a zone for aliens to land when they eventually arrive in our world during her lifetime. Despite her unconventional beliefs and unusual proclivities, I was drawn to her on a spiritual level. We spent the birthday party discussing our different callings to plant medicine. Katya started with mild psilocybin trips with friends and then a few years later graduated, or should I say elevated, to another stratosphere when she did ayahuasca while on a trip with friends in Las Vegas. Her experience with "mother aya," as Katya called it, was life-altering enough to trigger a years-long relationship with the plant medicine she now described as a "bitch."

"She puts me through the wringer every time," Katya said. She emerged from her first experience with ayahuasca convinced that her calling was to be a spiritual healer for others through psychedelics. Katya sought out and found a local shaman in Tucson, roughly a two-hour drive south of Phoenix. She underwent rigorous training for several years, observing the techniques of the shaman, who hailed from a small Peruvian village. She learned how to use ayahuasca, with ingredients shipped in from South America. She traveled to the source—the Peruvian city of Iquitos at the foot of the Amazon River. Over several weeks there, she studied and worked closely with local shamans while exploring her menu of psychedelic experiences.

She branched out along with learning more about perfecting the ayahuasca craft (how to make the tea, the proper chants, the best practices for timing it out, how to perform a ceremony, and so forth). She also tried kambo, a drug many call the new ayahuasca for its intense psychedelic properties. Ingesting kambo sounds like a form of Amazonian waterboarding. The legs of a giant monkey frog are tied up, forcing the animal to secrete venom to ward off predators. Your skin is then burned with a smoldering vine, and venom is placed on your body. The believers say it'll cure depression and give you a mean hard-on; there's no clinical evidence to back up these particular claims, but many celebrities and those entrenched in the psychedelic field swear by it.

Katya returned from the jungle and was encouraged in this new journey to become a medicine woman to others. Through word of mouth, she slowly built up a consistent base of clients in Phoenix and felt confident enough to officiate various psychedelic journeys regularly. She didn't limit herself to just performing ayahuasca ceremonies; she also worked with psilocybin, which she had received from some local growers, and MDMA, sent from Norway through a shockingly efficient way of getting drugs in the same classification as heroin and cocaine through the mail. She carved out an ample, fairly nondescript space off her living room in that Potter Drive house in North Phoenix as the location for these ceremonies. After years of practice, she was now a legitimate medicine woman. This is when I met her.

We both acknowledged that our meeting resulted from the universe's centrifugal forces bringing us together, but the question remained: Why? Then suddenly, and randomly, as I was swigging down a glass of watered-down iced chardonnay (the inner wine snob in me despises the ice, but it's a normal thing in Phoenix in the summer), Katya tapped me on the shoulder and said, "I think you should do an MD journey with me. I kinda feel like that's important for you."

At that point, my only experience with Molly had been a naked dance party on a beach maybe twenty years earlier. That is not how therapeutic ecstasy works, and as such, I was intrigued but apprehensive. "You can do Molly in a non-rave setting?" I asked.

"The difference," she said, "between the naked ecstasy party and the ones that are part of a psychedelic journey is the intention. It is the same drug; the only difference is why you embark on this journey."

This was an aha moment for me. I'd never thought about the purpose-driven drug experience.

"You must ask yourself why you're using these particular psychedelics, even Molly. It'll help with the journey you embark on," Katya said. I asked her when we could do an MD ceremony, and much to my surprise, she said, "How about Saturday?"

Five days later, I walked into that suburban North Phoenix ranch-style house for my first MDMA experience since Maui and the first time using it as a "journey." Katya had informed me to wear comfortable clothes, prepare for a six-hour trip, and plan to spend the night. I was reluctant to sleep over, as I usually require a room temperature cold enough to vaporize my breath. The ceremonial room was a toasty seventy-five degrees, aglow with a few candles next to Katya sitting on a yoga mat, covered by a small wool blanket.

About fifteen feet from her, at a ninety-degree angle, was another yoga mat and a series of blankets that resembled the soft childhood "blankies" many of us had as children and reluctantly relinquished as adolescence set in. I was fairly sure these animal-print covers had belonged to her now adult son and daughter. Next to the yoga mat on the left was a large water bottle (when you do ecstasy, you get thirsty quickly) as well as a pack of chewing gum (jaw clenching and teeth grinding are frequent side effects from Molly; some people even use pacifiers at raves to help offset it).

To my right was a small kitchen bowl lined with a plastic bag. "What's this for?" I asked. "Just in case you puke," was the response. I was perplexed, but Katya continued. "You never know. A lot of people have different reactions." I had not heard of people throwing up on MD, but then again, my system was sensitive enough for me to projectile vomit every time I tried smoking any form of weed.

After getting comfortable on my mat, I sat wondering what the next six-plus hours would be like.

What will we speak about for six hours?

How do I tell her there's no way I'm staying overnight in this hot box?

Seriously, what am I doing here?

My internal voice was having a field day. I wanted to see if this Molly was the magical elixir I recalled from twenty years earlier that may have tweaked my brain enough to help with my childhood abuse and PTSD. I wanted to know if using MDMA outside the realms of a recreational experience would be beneficial for my mental health. Ever since Hawaii, my trauma had moved into a portion of my brain that allowed me to be able to function with everyday life and experience some levels of romance and sexuality without triggering panic. It was no longer omnipresent, but I still wore that scarlet abuse scar deep in my soul. I just chose not to address it or have it impact my day to day. Perhaps it was the result of a small retweaking that took place once I'd had a positive romantic experience on MDMA. But little did I realize my excessive drinking, spiraling depression, and inability to maintain a long-term relationship—in any form—may have been negative responses to this trauma over the years.

Katya used her flashlight to carefully measure what appeared to be some crystals she pulled from a small sack. She walked over to me and placed 180 milligrams of pure MDMA in my hand, which I quickly swallowed. Later, I discovered that the dosage was on the high end of the "recommended" amount anyone should take on a trip, and it was just the first of two doses I would consume during this journey.

Now what?

I wondered about the purpose of this strictly platonic, inactive, somewhat sedative Molly experience.

"What are your intentions for this journey?" Katya whispered, her voice slightly louder than the massage parlor playlist blasting from a tiny JBL speaker. I didn't know my intentions except for wanting this experience to happen fast. It was warm, only the two of us, and I figured it would be boring. An hour into us sitting there, discussing our various psychedelic journeys, Katya asked me to explain why I was called to be there.

"I was sexually abused at a very young age by a teenage relative, and the first person I was infatuated with disappeared and died immediately following our first kiss, and I discovered his body." I continued, "I believe my first iteration with Molly helped me heal, and I hope this will continue that journey."

Katya was never formally trained as a therapist, but it was apparent she had acquired the same skills through her years of training as a medicine woman. Within minutes, I was revealing more on that yoga mat to this relative stranger than I ever had during my many attempts with traditional therapists.

As Katya transitioned from discussing heavy topics such as presidential politics to more mundane matters, tears began to flow, at times uncontrollably, from my eyes. There was no prevailing emotional thought to spur this particular purge. I wiped away the tears and hoped it wouldn't be evident to Katya, who was in the midst of a TED Talk discussing a myriad of topics, including how she would grow back her missing teeth and her plans for the alien landing strip. Despite her unconventional beliefs, there was something that had drawn me to Katya from the first time I met her. I couldn't quite place my finger on why I trusted to go on this journey with her, but I somehow knew she was the right person to take me safely through this experience. I felt drawn and comforted.

I lay back on my mat, staring at the ceiling. The tears slid down my face when suddenly my body started experiencing cold sweats. I had not eaten since breakfast some twelve hours prior, so the drug was moving through me quicker than expected. Katya started observing my body high, weighed an additional 20 mg of pure MDMA, and handed it to me. I couldn't help but wonder why she thought I wasn't high enough already.

"If it becomes too much, just tell the drug to back off," Katya reassured me. My hands were now sweaty and shaking from the effects of the drug as I moved the crystals closer to my mouth and swallowed them with a chaser of water.

I'm so high.

I was high, and not in the fun, party, Maui naked fire dance way I recalled from my previous trip on the drug. I was cold but sweating. I was trembling, my teeth were chattering, and there was Katya, asking me what makes me happy in life. I shrugged her off, waving my hands in hopes she would stop speaking. Her words and voice seemed to increase the nausea and exacerbate the high I was experiencing. I sat up on the mat in the yoga lotus position, with the cold sweat dripping from my forehead and my body swaying from a loss of control. I reached for the plastic bowl I initially thought would be useless. Then came that much too familiar sequence of events I would experience during my later psychedelic trips: my mouth began to water, followed by hiccups, followed by a quick succession of rapid-fire vomiting. I find this form of purging cathartic, partly because my body-dysmorphic split personality enjoyed the abdominal exercise and sense of weight loss that resulted from it.

"How are you feeling?" Katya asked as I lay back on the mat.

"I'm just really emotional right now, and I feel like I'm facing my trauma head-on."

As the drug moved through my body, it seemed to tap into parts of my mind I had stored away, an area where the deep-seated trauma sat. I vividly saw my relative's face and body as he crawled to my lower bunk that first night. My mind flashed between his image and Manny's; I could see the latter's pale arm, his hand in a fist, trapped in tree branches as the rapidly moving Belize River rippled around it. As the images of the funeral and my relative's repeated action flashed across my brain, my internal voice, faintly and repetitively, said, *Forgive*.

And again, *forgive*, over and over until I couldn't ignore it anymore and started whispering it aloud. Katya remained on her mat chanting an *icaro*. I would later learn about the power of these chants, words, and tunes, but as she described it, "The words and cadence can provide a portal to another world and engage your soul and the medicine." Her *icaro* included the words, "I release all that does not benefit me." For the first time during this session, I felt that my spiritual being and her output were on the same plane. Soon, that internal forgiving tone became my own, and those tears streamed down my face again. I said out loud:

"I forgive you."

I looked at the images of my relative streaming across the dark matter of my brain and said, "I forgive you, I forgive you." And then to Manny, as I relived our kiss and his tiny coffin, "I forgive you, Manny." My tear purge once again turned into a bawling cry, but I felt relief. For the first time in my life, I felt the importance of forgiving those who caused so much childhood trauma for me, and I gained comfort from it. I've always denied the actual impact it was having on my psyche, my mental health, and my ability to love others, and here I was able to confront it for the very first time.

A Turning Point

"Forgiving means not having to hold on. It was letting go because it only hurts you. By not forgiving, you suffer, because you think about it over and over."

—TINA TURNER

I recalled Tina Turner's quote about her abusive life as I left Katya's house in the predawn hours. I didn't spend the entire night, as I wanted to continue to resolve my experience by myself. The tears had long evaporated along with any hint of nausea. At that moment, I knew I had changed and had clarity that I would have to continue practicing forgiveness to keep the decades-long trauma from returning as a massive underlying weight on my mind, body, and actions. The PTSD that haunted me for so many decades manifested itself by allowing my childhood abuse and scars to weigh me down. That force had now been lifted.

I called Dr. McCowan once more to get his assessment following my journey in Arizona. "Joseph, I felt I had a breakthrough in which I forgave my relative and Manny. Does that make sense?" I asked him.

"Absolutely," he said. "I'm happy to hear this is what you've experienced. This drug allows us to not only confront traumatic demons, it allows us to come to terms with them. Often, forgiveness, compassion, and self-love are the flowers of this synthetic plant medicine."

I knew he was right. My MDMA experience in Arizona had reinforced the feeling I'd had in Hawaii so many years earlier and had finally given me some form of comfort over the demons from my childhood.

CHAPTER 4

Trip Two: LSD

There's a reason they add the word "panic" to these sorts of attacks. The Mayo Clinic describes them as "sudden episode[s] of intense fear that [trigger] severe physical reactions when there is no real danger or apparent cause." Perhaps with the added context of said panic attack taking place on live television during your network morning television debut, they'd probably add "crapping your pants" as a descriptor.

My first panic attack hit on November 20, 2010, shortly after 7:08 a.m. eastern standard time. (Do you get a sense it still burns an indelible hole in my brain?)

I've always had a playlist to hype me up before a broadcast. Most songs are uplifting and motivational, and there's the occasional fight song and Eminem's award-winning hit "Lose Yourself." Picture me blasting it in my dressing room on my trusty speaker, rapping along with Em. But when a panic attack decides to crash the party, those lyrics take on a whole new vibe—specifically his words about sweaty palms, weak knees, and heavy arms.

Except there's *no* "snap back to reality" when you're entirely panicked. I was speaking about then president Barack Obama's trip to a NATO meeting. I had to get through a fifteen-second script and hand it off to a live reporter, and I couldn't make it. I was the only person on camera with millions of people watching and observing my every word and move. I stumbled over "this morning" and suddenly paused, staring into the camera lens, unable to comprehend the words in the teleprompter in plain English in front of me. At that moment, I was alone in the studio. The room temperature had suddenly dropped to freezing, yet I was sweating. There was no floor director, who seconds earlier had directed me to look into camera two, no nearby anchors on the half-circle white couch, no one in my ear. It was just me, the black-and-white camera screen, and those blurred-out words.

With more than three million viewers watching, it couldn't have come at a worse time. But more importantly for me, the moment was essentially an on-air audition, with several top network executives focused on my performance with future star potential in mind. I had worked so hard to get to this point in my career, and within fifteen seconds, it was over.

Freaking Out Over Beyoncé...and Not in a Good Way

Beyoncé looked like a golden goddess, sitting inches away from me, making small talk, hoping the microphones wouldn't pick up what she was saying. She wasn't the BEYONCÉ of today, but she was well on her way to becoming an icon with an immeasurable aura about her. She sat there, her posture admirably upright, wearing gold from head to toe. Her hair was now pulled back into large curls in a mod updo circa the 1960s, and she rocked a sweetheart neckline with intricate beading and a layered gold silk dress. I was thankful for my producer, Rosemary, who provided the proper adjectives to describe Beyoncé's fashion statement that evening. We were at the

Staples Center, as the arena was named at the time, in a CNN suite specially decorated for us to interview the stars, and that night we were promised to be Beyoncé's first interview stop after she left the Grammy stage. I had spent years cultivating a relationship with the future legend and her team, so much so that they opted to meet with me first before any national television network outlet or one of the syndicated entertainment television shows.

The interview was scheduled to be brief—five minutes total—but I had to cut it even shorter and wrap the sit-down after only two minutes. It was my third time interviewing the emerging icon in three years, yet this was the most nervous I had ever been. About ninety minutes earlier, I had rushed through the halls in a panic. This night was supposed to be a massive boost for my career at CNN. I had been at the network for two years and, through my contacts, navigated some major entertainment "gets," especially for a young correspondent based in Atlanta, far from the hubbub of Hollywood or New York. I was working the early morning show at the sister network, HLN. It was the second time in my career that I was working early hours, and it was quickly becoming clear the shift was exacerbating my underlying mental health problems. On-air, I had mild heart palpitations and brain zaps that caused occasional stumbles. I never knew if there was a diagnosis for what I was experiencing and never went to a doctor about it.

Just a day ahead of the forty-sixth annual Grammy Awards in Los Angeles, I traveled from Atlanta with my producer, Rosemary Jean-Louis, a frail, diminutive, but brilliant entertainment industry visionary. She was also highly proficient at providing for every need I would have to ensure we put on the best segment and be able to shine. In this case, I desperately needed a good night's sleep after working the early shift, flying cross-country, and prepping for our early call time to do our morning segment three hours earlier than usual. Before crashing for the night, Rosemary offered me the sleep aid Ambien, which would be my first time taking one.

As I have learned over my career, producers, bookers, and even agents will provide whatever downers or uppers you need to be your best self on-air or during important interviews. Thanks to the 10 mg pill with a chaser of minibar chardonnay, I crashed as the sun set on the West Coast. My body clock, however, was still on East Coast time, and I "woke up" three hours later and walked to the bathroom, still in a haze. I don't recall where exactly I relieved myself, but my true awakening came as I stood outside my room wearing nothing but boxer briefs, shaking the doorknob, and trying to get back inside. I had to perform the ultimate walk of shame shirtless (fortunately, I had been on a low-carb diet) and got to the front desk of the Best Western hotel, with a lobby just steps from busy Sunset Boulevard. I'm still unsure if there was a tinge of sarcasm as the hotel clerk asked if I was carrying any identification, but they eventually took my word for it. Unsurprisingly, I could not get back to sleep once I returned to my room. It was 1:00 a.m. I was wide awake, had to be on-air in two hours, and was expected to stay up through the end of the awards show that evening. I was royally screwed.

Between the lack of sleep, the Ambien that was still running through my veins, and the countereffects of several hundred milligrams of caffeine I had consumed throughout the day, my nerves were completely shot by the time the Grammys kicked off that night. Prince, dressed in his trademark purple suit, walked down a flight of stage stairs as the show began before diving into a few bars of "Purple Rain" while accompanied by a large symphony.

At that moment, I was having a panic attack and rushing from the CNN green room to the nearest toilet outside the suite so I wouldn't attract too much attention. It all seemed a blur at the time—the parade of stars who occupied that floor mingling with journalists and publicists. I brushed past a young Kanye West, just two days from the release of his freshman album, *The College Dropout*, and overheard an MTV veejay (when that was still a thing) praising what a great piece of work he had produced. I flew by Matthew McConaughey at a stand-alone cocktail table by himself while hoping not to throw up on the way to the bathroom, barely making it in time to projectile vomit all over the walls.

I sat on my knees in a brand-new dark blue suit, hugging the toilet. My heart was pounding loud enough to hear it beating outside my body. My vision had become blurry, I could barely breathe, and my entire body was covered with sweat. I could hear Beyoncé join Prince on the Grammy stage for the second verse of "Purple Rain." She was experiencing a pivotal moment in her young career, and I was hugging a toilet in the midst of a panic attack.

I stood up carefully and washed my hands, scared to look into the mirror and confront the frightening state of my face. Shockingly, except for bloodshot eyes, I looked okay. I washed my face and tried taking calming breaths, inhaling deeply and exhaling a few times. It did little to calm my nerves, but it gave me time to gather myself.

I returned to our green room, where my producers and camera crew were set up and waiting for me to interview other award winners from that evening. Always prepared, Rosemary leaned over and whispered, "Would you like some eyedrops?" I acquiesced. And from there, it was off to the races, from one artist to another. There was little time for nerves, but the panic was simmering just beneath the surface.

My palms were still somewhat sweaty as Beyoncé walked into our suite. Luckily, we had such a level of familiarity by this point that I could skip a handshake for a brief hug. I was already seated, and our camera team was ready to roll when she sat down for our scheduled five-minute interview. After a bit of chitchat not intended for the cameras or microphones, I realized, *Oh shit*, I hadn't seen her performance with Prince because of my anxiety attack. *What will I ask her?*

I started with a hard-hitting question that would have made Barbara Walters proud:

"Performing with Prince—wha wha wha was that like?"

"I can't believe it," she responded in the thickest Houston accent anyone could imagine. "I can't believe I was on the stage singing in one mic with Prince. I mean, it's unbelievable; he's such an inspiration."

I managed to ask one more question about her returning to the studio with Destiny's Child. As she responded to my question, my mouth started watering, and the more I swallowed, the more I felt the urge to throw up. Suddenly, my nausea was compounded by a zap to my brain, and I knew I had to cut this interview short.

Bey looked slightly surprised when I said, "Thank you," and reached over to shake her hand, still sweaty from my panic attack. I turned my back to her, rushed out of the room, and headed to the bathroom again, trying to hide the tears streaming down my face. It was the biggest night of my career at that point, and I had spent a large part of it puking, riddled with anxiety and panic.

My colleagues could tell that something was up, and my co-anchor Robin Meade, who publicly discussed her anxiety as a local news anchor, came to my office a few days later and urged me to talk to someone. She recommended a therapist in Chicago, where she had previously worked.

The therapist confirmed that I was suffering from panic attacks, explained how it was a side effect of my overall depression, and recommended I see someone local in Atlanta who could prescribe selective serotonin reuptake inhibitors, or SSRIs, to reduce my issues. I was so afraid in those days that my mental health diagnosis would be leaked and have a negative impact on my burgeoning career that I was hesitant to see a doctor, so I consulted with one of the network's on-air medical professionals, Dr. Sandra Fryhofer. First, I was prescribed Wellbutrin, but after three months of increasing dosage, I found it did very little for my mood. I romanticized jumping off my thirtieth-floor Atlanta apartment balcony, and my on-air anxiety brain zaps returned. Dr. Fryhofer suggested I switch to Zoloft, a popular antidepressant in the class of SSRIs, which increases serotonin levels in the brain and improves moods.

After three months on the medication, I found that my mood had elevated, my teary-eyed nights were a thing of the past, and, most importantly, my anxiety attacks and brain zaps had all but disappeared. I could focus on my performance and being present for my friends and family. But during the several years I took the SSRI, I noticed an emergent problem—I may not have experienced the daily despair, but because those emotions weren't being treated by therapy, they didn't go away. I would still suffer explosions of the underlying issues, occasionally erupting in the most profound sorrow I've ever experienced, and the most epic of panic attacks.

Panic On the Studio Floor

In the summer of 2010, I arrived at CBS News as a Los Angeles–based correspondent for its affiliate service, CBS Newspath. I was the correspondent whose stories would be national filler in local newscasts. Don't get me wrong, it was a significant honor to be working at a network, but at the same time, I was the bitch boy for local stations across the country who called the shots on what to say, what stories I covered, how to do them, and even what to wear. When I was covering the anniversary of Hurricane Katrina in ninety-five-degree heat and soaring humidity in late-August New Orleans, I got a call from the office of the then all-powerful news director of WCBS television, David Friend, after one of my earlier live reports for his station. In addition to his executive powers, apparently Friend was also the head of the CBS fashion police.

"David isn't happy with the Polo shirt and jeans you're wearing," I was told. "You need to get a suit." Despite his last name, he was a friend to very few in the television business, especially people of color.

And so, on the 5:00 p.m. newscast that same day, I stood on top of a levee in the Ninth Ward in a navy-blue suit and knee-high yellow boots. I was not only suffocating from the heat and humidity in that suit, my ego was also dying because I looked like a complete idiot. But what goes around comes around, and eventually, David Friend was unceremoniously dismissed after years of complaints about his abusive and, in many cases, racist behavior toward employees.

I had some big backers in New York who had recruited me: Barbara Fedida, the senior vice president of news who oversaw the talent department, and her second in charge, Mary Noonan, a former CBS *48 Hours* producer turned talent executive, both of whom would play a significant role in my television news career spanning several national networks and years. From my early days at CBS, it was clear that Newspath was just a point of entry into the network; Katie Couric met with me personally to assure me there were bigger plans afoot for me, as did her executive producer, the legendary network man Rick Kaplan, who once imparted this singular piece of sage career advice to me: During a hurricane or storm, always wear an oversize coat several times larger than your body so the wind will appear more epic than the reality. So, when I got a call from Mary in early November, after only a few months on the job, I figured the plan was underway.

"We'd like you to come to New York over the Thanksgiving holiday to fill in as the newsreader on *The Early Show*." I ran to the bathroom at the CBS Studio Center lot, screaming to myself, Michael Scott from *The Office* style:

"Oh my *gawd*, okay, it's happening. Stay calm!"

Despite all being under one roof, network shows and divisions operate differently, with each concerned only about its own individual needs. On the Friday before my *Early Show* debut, I still had to perform my regular duties doing live reports and something we called "sig outs" for the dozens of TV stations nationwide.

"In Los Angeles, Kendis Gibson, CBS 2, New York."

"In Los Angeles, Kendis Gibson, Hawaii News Now."

"In Los Angeles, Kendis Gibson, KENS 5 Eyewitness News."

"In Los Angeles, Kendis Gibson, KYW Eyewitness News."

You'd be surprised how many stations nationwide are eyewitnesses to the news. Some days, based on the popularity of your story, your list of sign outs could be near one hundred. Luckily, it was only about a dozen on that Friday, and I was cut loose relatively early to make a noon flight that would get me into New York's JFK airport by 9:00 p.m.

I rushed from the airport to Macy's Herald Square to get an outfit to make an exclamation statement on television. I bought a nearly $500 camel-colored winter coat and hit up the Hugo Boss department for a checkered purple-and-white shirt and matching purple tie. If I were dressing for my NBA draft day selection, this would have been the perfect outfit; little did I know then that basics are the way to go. The bosses would later inform me that less is more in television news fashion. I ended up closing Macy's that evening, rushed to my hotel, and stopped briefly at the lobby bar for a Manhattan cocktail made neatly (I figured it would be appropriate). I was so exhausted from travel and a lack of sleep, I found myself rolling along the walls of my hotel, barely making it to my room and bed before passing out.

The call time for the car service is 4:00 a.m. for a newscast starting three hours later. It was obvious to me as I climbed into that SUV at the Essex House hotel on Central Park South for the brief drive to CBS's General Motors Building that I was still fucked up from the sleeping pill I had taken less than six hours prior. I walked into the General Motors Building on the southeast corner of Central Park and tried to overcome my imposter syndrome. Yes, I deserved to have a producer devoted totally to my segment.

"Mr. Gibson, would you like water?"

Mister?! Okay, I thought.

"Ahem, yeah, sure."

"Sparkling or still?"

"New York tap?"

As the producer escorted me to the makeup room, I walked by the array of free breakfast sandwiches, sweets, and bagels; in local news, you get free food only twice a year, on Thanksgiving and election nights. I sat down in the makeup chair and was handed newspaper clippings and the script for the two minutes of airtime I would be responsible for. I thought this would be a cakewalk; instead, they were the two longest minutes of my life.

The first indication that something was wrong came as I read the clippings and script. Reading was fine; comprehending seemed to be a different matter. I read and reread the same newspaper articles and script several times as my makeup artist applied extra concealer to hide the dark circles and lines that would easily expose my lack of sleep. I didn't understand anything I was reading. After placing my earpiece and microphone on, I quietly conducted breathing exercises, but I'm pretty sure I wasn't doing them correctly. I inhaled to a four count:

One, two, three, four...

And exhaled, counting down in my head, back to one:

Four, three, two, one.

And again, and again. It wasn't making a difference.

I noticed my heart was still pounding heavily and hard. I put my right hand inside my suit jacket pretending to be adjusting my shirt, but instead I wanted to see if I could feel the pounding outside my chest. I could. Being conscious of my breath wasn't necessarily an exercise but instead focused my brain on what could be wrong.

Has the Adderall kicked in yet?

I'm so tired.

I just need to get through the next hour of television and only two two-minute segments.

My mind was starting to race.

I tried to grab the glass of water in the CBS *The Early Show* mug that had been placed in front of me. My hand was shaking so much as I lifted the mug I decided to put it back down so I wouldn't give away to the control room that something was wrong.

"Good morning, Kendis. How are you?" the executive producer interrupted my inner self-sabotage. "We are so excited to have you join us. Knock 'em dead."

Gulp.

Going from Newspath to *The Early Show* was the TV news equivalent of a baseball prospect being called up from the minors. The gravity of this moment weighed heavily on me as I strode to the single anchor standing desk between the main anchor set and the weather wall. The anchors, Rebecca Jarvis and Chris Wragge, would toss over to me, and then I would toss to the weather person, Lonnie Quinn.

Continue to breathe.

I kept telling myself to stay calm, but it wasn't working. Fifteen seconds into my read, I had already stumbled and had a pregnant pause. I could feel the sweat beads above my lip. I successfully made it to the reporter handoff. It gave me ninety seconds to breathe, gather my thoughts, and compose myself.

The show's executive producer got in my earpiece out of concern. "Are you okay?"

I wasn't okay.

"Yeah, just got a little warm at the top of the segment here in the studio," I lied.

"Want me to get them to lower the studio temperatures a little?"

"Sure, that would be nice," I responded, assuming it would take several minutes to control a building's temperature on a weekend morning, and perhaps it would give me an excuse in case things didn't improve in the next few minutes. My heart rate only intensified, compounded by a shortness of breath.

I was back on camera following the slight reprieve from the dispatch from our correspondent traveling with the president in Portugal.

"Bill, thank you. A letter…" I stumbled and paused, inhaling, then continued. "…containing white powder was received last night in Los Angeles." Thankfully, it was time for another reporter package (a full report all on tape lasting at least a minute). I drank some water once I handed it off to that reporter, my hands visibly shaking as the glass reached my mouth. For five excruciating minutes, the pattern would continue from there. I read, I stumbled, I paused, and continued. After six stumbles and pregnant pauses during my segment, I could finally hand off to Lonnie Quinn, who is a burst of energy on an average day. On this particular morning, the difference in energy and confidence couldn't have been more stark. Lonnie took the baton from me quickly, before I was even done mindlessly bantering about some early Christmas decorations in Opryland.

I walked off set, fully realizing that my star trajectory was over. The panic attack that seconds earlier had consumed every element of my body had suddenly dissipated. My breathing, which seemed suffocating moments earlier, had stabilized. My heart was pounding at a more normal rate, and the moisture that covered my hands was starting to dry up. But I still didn't think I was able to muster an ad-lib off the top of my head without having some sort of mental spasm.

I walked over to the curved couch where all the anchors gathered at the bottom of the hour to chitchat about mindless watercooler topics and felt utterly numb. Rebecca and Chris had a gaze of concern for my well-being. Fortunately, I didn't have to face them once we went off-air because I rushed to the airport for an early morning flight back to the West Coast. I spoke with the network executives, including the head of talent, the following Monday, and while they did not bring up the situation, they acknowledged to my agent it was not my strongest performance and didn't live up to expectations. I was never given an opportunity at filling again, and the plans for me becoming a full-blown CBS network correspondent never came to pass.

I needed to get help with these panic attacks, but I didn't know how. I hated therapy, I was already on SSRIs, and I felt that I had no way of correcting my situation.

Big Sur, Bad LSD

I developed a really close group of friends during my days as an anchor and reporter in San Diego. Three of them I met as coworkers at FOX 5 San Diego where I had been anchoring the primetime newscasts, as well as my friend Prince, who eventually played a large role in my plant medicinal journey. We made road trips together, went to clubs as a unit, and partied hard. Those boys never saw a drug they didn't try and, in most cases, liked. I, on the other hand, was not fond of experimenting with illegal narcotics. My friends tried everything to get me up to their level. They forced me to try weed, and I'd cough for the next half hour after one puff. They hot-boxed me in my bathroom, where the entire group smoked weed, anticipating I'd get a contact high. It worked, and I spent the next hour in the said bathroom puking. We tried weed gummies, which left me in the corner of a party in La Jolla in the fetal position, begging for my mommy and wishing the gummy would exorcise my body.

Then one day they suggested another illegal drug solution for my panic attacks: LSD. My only previous exposure to acid came during my junior year at SUNY Oswego, when my roommate, Dan Lyons, would spend entire Saturday evenings and, in some cases, Sunday mornings, tripping, sometimes for up to twelve hours.

I always marveled at how a small piece of paper, laced with a drop of liquid, could provide so much entertainment (he spent hours staring at the colors of *Simpsons* episodes on TV), exhaustion, and sexual arousal. I never imagined it would be presented as a solution for my anxiety attacks and depression.

Although acid had been in use for decades, the research and jury were still out on the benefits of this Schedule 1 illegal drug in terms of its impact on depression and panic attacks. After much discussion and a massive pressure campaign from my friends, I capitulated and agreed to try it.

We lived in Southern California, but few of us had ever been to Big Sur, the rugged coastline about two and a half hours south of San Francisco. The area has some of the most epic hiking trails in the country, many of which are lined with breathtaking waterfalls. Matt, the nerdier planner of the group, selected a trail in Limekiln State Park within the Big Sur area, perfectly mapping out when the acid would hit as we arrived at a picturesque waterfall vista.

Our crew set out early one September morning in 2011 in a small Toyota Camry rental the boys had picked up in San Diego. My friend Prince—and perhaps this should have been my first red flag—had bought the tiny Flintstones-decorated acid paper tabs from a guy across the border in Tijuana, Mexico, named Josh—pretty sketchy sounding, but we were too happy to get our hands on the product to worry about it. We decided to take a rental car just in case we got stopped and searched (there were two minorities in the vehicle, after all). That plan got tested early in our ride, as the boys had smoked up the car with weed in another veiled attempt to hot-box me and give me a contact high, and we were pulled over by highway patrol just north of Oxnard, California, on the I-5.

"License and registration."

Prince, of Indian descent, and me, a prime candidate for racial profiling, sat there shitting bricks, worried that we would get locked up for the massive stash of weed in the glove compartment. California was still several years away from legalizing pot, and no one in the car had a medical marijuana card. And then there was the matter of those highly illicit acid tabs hidden in a toiletry kit. Matt, our tall White skater-slash-hipster Wisconsin-bred friend, had been driving 90 miles an hour in a 65-mph zone. Perhaps it was privilege on display that, despite the lingering smell of that high-grade kush, the officer allowed Matt to drive off with a simple warning and "Be careful." And a mere thirty miles north on the same highway, we were again pulled over for speeding. This time, Matt got a ticket, but there was no search of the vehicle, and we resumed our journey in our contraband-packed Camry.

Limekiln State Park, along the Big Sur Coast Highway, seemed the perfect place for us to hike and trip our asses off for several hours. Prince told me to keep my thoughts positive, as any negative notions could lead to a bad trip and being stuck in it for hours—a concept which in and of itself gave me added anxiety.

I thought LSD was supposed to alleviate my panic attacks and chill my nerves?!

The park sits on 700 acres of formerly industrial land used to harvest limestone more than a century ago. It boasts a relatively easy 1.5-mile hike to the main attractions, majestic falls, and some relic kilns. Matt figured few people would be on the trail, and it would be the perfect place to commune with nature.

Before leaving the parking lot, he handed each of us one of the acid tabs placed in the lining of his toiletry bag. They were clear, didn't have a smell, and were about the size of the top of my index finger and reminded me of those cool mint breath strips of paper. It barely touched my tongue before I could taste a slight bitter tap in the middle of the square, and within a second of my saliva rushing in from both sides of my mouth onto the paper, it was gone. There was no turning back from there. Matt figured we had twenty to thirty minutes before the fun began.

We walked along a small creek-lined trail, with few people visible and dwarfed by towering redwood trees. Our heads turned nearly horizontal to peer at their crowns. The boys smoked a few trees of their own as we slowly wandered toward the waterfall a mile away. My heart was increasingly fluttering along this minimal-difficulty trail; my nerves were in overdrive. Perhaps Prince was correct in his conclusion that the Swiss chemist who first synthesized the drug in the 1930s did it no favors by including "acid" in its name. It made for a frightening concept for me despite all the positive appraisals of the substance. Yet, I was so desperate for anything that could help with my anxiety that even if something didn't have a focus group-approved moniker, I was willing to give it a shot.

Our stroll through the forest took a little longer than we anticipated, partly due to the revelation that you shouldn't go on a hike with a group of people who've smoked a shit ton of weed. After forty-five laborious minutes, we arrived at the Limekiln waterfalls, a breathtaking stream reaching nearly one hundred feet into the air. I'm not sure if I was already under the drug's spell or nature's sorcery, but I was mesmerized by the beauty of life at that very moment. I crawled over to a dry slab of limestone at the base of a small pool of water created by the falls. I sat there, looking at the environment around me, marveling and in awe of the beauty, waiting and wondering if this would be the beginning of the end of my panic attacks, which, at that moment, had the potential to ruin a career I had worked so hard to achieve.

Matt had set a timer from when we took the acid to know when it would likely take effect and how much longer we would have to remain on the trip. It had now been two and a half hours, and still, there was no discernible effect on us. The boys suggested moving around would let the chemical take hold a little more quickly. We did jumping jacks, ran back and forth from both banks of the waterfall, and did some leg lifts. Any strangers walking nearby would suspect we were either doing some weird cult-indoctrinating ritualistic dance or on drugs. Unfortunately at this point, it was neither.

There was no altered sensation manifesting through our bodies. Our minds were clear but not clairvoyant. Our vision was more holistic than hallucinogenic. Our senses were far from overstimulated—the acid tablets were fake.

In a way, I was relieved because I was already reluctant to spend up to twelve hours on an acid high. As we made our way back to the car, Matt put his hand on my shoulder. "I'm sorry, buddy," he said. There was uniform disappointment among our crew, partly because they were hoping to get an epic ten-hour high amid California's paradise, but also because they wanted this as a possible solution to my problems. Instead, we jumped back in our car, feeling as sober as when we'd left the vehicle, with an added dose of dissatisfaction and frustration.

Plant Whisperer

William Padilla-Brown was just nine years old when he had his first psychedelic experience after smoking some intense cannabis that he got from his classmates. It was the start of an essentially love/hate relationship with psychedelics (he considers cannabis to be in this category because of the psychoactive effects he gets while smoking weed). Upon meeting him, most people might not be too surprised to learn that Padilla-Brown is into weed and psychedelics. He has a laid-back demeanor, embracing all of life's gifts, as if he had just taken a puff of the strongest marijuana strain. He's a light-skinned brotha with the sort of soft, long dreadlocks that even Bob Marley would envy.

Padilla-Brown's experimentation with drugs wasn't limited to the greater Harrisburg, Pennsylvania, area, where he lived; he traveled the world with his father, who was an army contractor. "I was trying to achieve a different state of consciousness everywhere I went," he says. One of these included a near out-of-body psychedelic experience seventy-nine feet aboveground on top of the main temple in Chichén Itzá, the popular Mayan ruin located in Mexico's Yucatan Peninsula. "I was thirteen years old and felt like I was sitting on top of my first Lego set. I kept looking around and saw so many years in the future in alignment and kept wondering how people could just take pictures here and not see and feel the energy I was experiencing."

After that, his young journey with psychedelics hit overdrive, and by age sixteen, he smoked the extremely hallucinogenic psychedelic kambo that's made from scraping venom off a particular species of frog. It produces an intense twenty-minute experience that can allegedly cure everything from social anxiety to severe depression (personally, as bad as my depression got, I just couldn't see myself inhaling vaporized frog sweat). William then dropped out of high school with the belief that he could learn much more through the chemical experiences he was having and his worldwide travels.

Upon returning to central Pennsylvania, he started foraging for mushrooms in the forest and cultivating his own magic mushrooms. Then he had his first LSD experience at age seventeen. "It was life changing," he told me. Unlike the failed sour-tasting Flintstones tab that I had in Big Sur, his had a neutral taste (which he said means it's the real thing), was in the pure liquid form of drops that he placed on his tongue, and actually worked.

For nearly twelve hours, he flew through space, experienced time bending, and watched shapes shifting in front of his eyes. During his trip, William met his newborn son well more than a year before his child was conceived and born. Along the course of the journey, he said he found his mission: spread the word of plant medicine and cultivation throughout the world. He found a unique niche industry that straddled the fungi fence between legal mushrooms and magic mushrooms. He taught himself mycology and launched a company called MycoSymbiotics, which teaches people how to forage, cultivate, and extract all forms of mushrooms.

I sought him out some time after my busted Big Sur acid experience on the recommendations of friends who were familiar with his extensive work in the psychedelic space. My friends knew I remained curious as to whether LSD could be a solution for some of my panic attack issues. I wondered whether another drug primarily used recreationally could help me.

My first mistake, William said, was "getting it from some random dude in Tijuana." *No shit*, I thought. "I now have testing kits, because before people used to give me stuff that tasted nasty and I knew it wasn't real," he told me. "It's best to get it in liquid form and put it in a breath dropper so you're able to measure it out. One hundred micrograms is probably a beginner dose."

I appreciated the intel, but I wasn't seeking a go-to guide on how to use acid. It had long been associated with hippies, and I had such reluctance to do drugs, as a former church boy and Bible-toting Christian well into my twenties (most people who know me now will find this statement utterly unbelievable). I wanted to hear from a Black expert, and despite his biracial tones, I knew William could be that expert, one who would help me determine whether LSD could, in essence, save my television career and eliminate the panic attacks.

"LSD is an antidepressant," William said, "and it really gives us the mental capacity to dive into the root causes of our problems, especially if you give yourself time to just sit with it. That's brought about my most powerful experiences." He said the setting is very important and that the last thing I want to be is "out on some hike in the forest with some animals around and a bunch of tourists walking, while I'm tripping balls." I asked him about his own preferred environment for LSD use. "I usually sit in my home," he said, "with a bunch of crystal around the space, have the lights turned down nicely, while burning some incense, and I have food and water nearby, because I don't want to be bugging anyone or have them bother me." He got me intrigued, and it sounded like our Big Sur plan was a bad idea from the start due to the environment.

"So, you think I could really benefit from it with these panic attacks?"

"Panic attacks are a form of anxiety, which are in the same mental health family as depression, and it has been shown to help with the latter." I started to metaphorically lean into the discussion, nearly to a level of impulse. "Studies have shown," he said, "that LSD can improve mood disturbances and as such reduce anxiety following a trip, But"—*uh-oh*—"and it's a big 'but,' in certain people LSD can induce panic attacks."

From a television news standpoint, this is what we'd call burying the lede: USING LSD TO TREAT PANIC ATTACKS COULD TRIGGER MORE PANIC ATTACKS. "You've heard of people having a 'bad trip,' right? Well, those are often caused by the individual panicking over a sight, sound, or spiritual element and reverting to a panic attack." Given the length of some acid trips, the idea of having a panic attack while under the influence sounded like the worst thing that could possibly happen. My band of California misfits who were just experimenting in the psychedelic space willy-nilly, while well intentioned, could have possibly made my situation worse.

I was appreciative of William's insight and knowledge in the space, but I was worried that LSD would not be a solution I could turn to for anything that ailed me. I realized the science regarding LSD's efficacy with panic attacks was in the very early research stages, and many of those convinced of its impact in this space were sourcing a cross between Wikipedia and Urban Dictionary. I pursued this particular drug trip because I was convinced it could be an out of the box idea that could help salvage an increasingly impactful problem on my performance. I never got that answer in regard to LSD. It would, however, come in the form of another psychedelic.

CHAPTER 5

Trip Three: ABC, Belize, and Psilocybin

There's an old description from an anonymous producer about what it's like to work for the big three television networks. "The walls of 30 Rockefeller Plaza," he said, describing the NBC headquarters, "are lined with sweat, because they'll work you to death. The walls at 57 West 57th where CBS is located, are lined with tears, because it's so depressing working there, and the walls at 67 West 66th [home to ABC] are lined with blood from all the backstabbing that takes place there." I spent many days busting a lot of sweat, tears, and blood while at ABC News. On the night of October 12, my eyes were still fairly swollen from all the tears I cried as I went into the office. I walked in around 11:00 p.m. that evening, closed my door, and skipped the normal midnight meeting to save my energy for the show, which began taping shortly after 1:00 a.m. each weekday.

I'd always wanted this job. More than a decade earlier, I first started watching it while Anderson Cooper was hosting *World News Now*, and after I reached out to him for insight on the program, he offered to give me a tour of the set. I was anchoring in Washington, DC, in the fall of 2014, when Mary Noonan, who was now a vice president of talent development, called to say they'd like to hire me as a correspondent at ABC News and it would include some anchoring on the overnight show. I couldn't have been any happier. I was originally hired as a correspondent for the Washington, DC, bureau, but first I headed to New York for my orientation, training, and welcoming, which included a heartwarming reception from Robin Roberts, Michael Strahan, and George Stephanopoulos on the set of *GMA*.

"We would like to welcome the newest member of the *Good Morning America* family, Kendis Gibson," said Robin, as the entire studio erupted in applause. I had already appeared on *GMA* the week before, but this was the official anointing by the queen of the show. She couldn't have been nicer and more genuine on and off camera, especially one day when I brought my mother to the set. My mother was sitting in the corner of the Times Square studio taking pictures of Robin and George with her oversize iPad when Robin quietly whispered for the director to get a shot of my mom once we came back from my story. We came back on camera, and before moving on to the next story Robin said, "Thanks for bringing your mom to work with you." The color dropped from my face—I was equal parts horrified and happy. I just hoped Mom didn't say anything to embarrass me. In the end, she barely realized she was on camera because her head was buried behind the iPad, paying very little attention to the TV screens or what was happening in the studio. We laughed, and I was able to breathe again.

After a few weeks in New York doing orientation, I was sent off for my first assignment, and ironically enough it was not in Washington, DC. Despite having an office with my nameplate waiting for me there, I never set foot in the DC bureau. Instead, I went west to Las Vegas for a shoot for *Nightline* that featured a behind-the-scenes view of ESPN's "The Body Issue," which featured athletes posing naked. In this particular case, it was a gift from the gods as I got to watch baseball superstar Bryce Harper pose in the buff for an entire day at a facility just off the Strip. He was just coming off one of his best seasons on the field and had spent his time away from the diamond getting into the best shape of his life. If this was an omen for how my career at ABC would go, I had literally died and gone to heaven.

I was then assigned to be a correspondent based in Los Angeles, which got off to an ominous start when I was assaulted by a homeless man following my first *World News Tonight* live report on skid row. The producer's and photographer's main focus was to make sure the homeless guy didn't continue swinging and possibly break the $10,000 camera; none seemed to express any concern about *my* well-being. I ran to my car rental and bawled my eyes out.

I ended up spending another five months working out of our West Coast bureau, covering everything from wildfires to oil spills, hurricanes in Texas, the occasional celebrity trash, and even the riots in Ferguson, Missouri. After my skid row incident, I asked the assignment desk for security to join me during the riots, which they agreed to pay for. But once our team of retired law enforcement guys arrived and we walked through the gauntlet of store fires and bottles thrown in every direction during one of the biggest nights of rioting, it was clear my personal safety was not their concern. My understanding was they were told to be there to make sure none of the equipment got damaged or stolen.

I was beginning to sense a pattern: ABC had a fascinating way of valuing individual lives. There was an unwritten but well-vocalized rule at the assignment desk in New York that dictated whether a story would be covered. Perhaps it was discussed and repeated in jest, but it reflected the stories the network chose to report in those days. The rule, as told to me by an ABC correspondent and echoed by a producer, both people of color: if there was an American casualty, it most likely would get some sort of mention or story. From there, according to them, the rule stated that each American life equaled two Canadian lives, three British lives, ten European lives, and from there, the numbers jumped exponentially. It often required dozens of Asians and hundreds of Africans before a story got the same level of coverage as that one American's death.

"Lifestyles of the Rich...and Kendis"

I remained in the West Coast bureau as the ultimate utility player willing to do everything and go anywhere. Then suddenly, the call I wanted came. T. J. Holmes, who had been anchoring the overnight show, was too sick to handle the hours and, by way of a doctor's and lawyer's note, had requested to be taken off the show immediately. Within twenty-four hours, T. J. was removed from the overnight anchor desk and I was packing my bags for New York City for the foreseeable future. Nearly three years later, as my health started to deteriorate while working the show, I wasn't afforded the same luxury to come off the program.

World News Now was one of those quirky news shows that I swear the bosses never watched, or we would have been fired long ago. It was a mix of news, sports, pop culture, lots of dancing, and lots of food and drinking. Our viewers consisted mostly of nursing moms, college students pulling all-nighters, third shifters, late-night partiers—we did not judge. I was initially paired with Reena Ninan, who had come over from FOX News, where she had been a no-nonsense Middle East correspondent. Despite the fact that David Muir, Anderson Cooper, Juju Chang, and a lot of reputable, tough journalists did this program, it was definitely not that type of show when I arrived.

Some six months into my tenure, the network hired Diane Macedo from the local CBS station to anchor the program. In the first segment when we were learning more about Diane's background and introducing her to the audience, she goes, "And that's just the tip!" At which point we both burst into laughter and the show mercifully cut to a preprogrammed commercial break. We were dying laughing while also cringing, wondering, *Are we going to get fired?* Thankfully we weren't, and it was off to the races from there.

It was an amazing pairing. Diane and I loved singing, dancing, and laughing on- and off-air. We routinely bounced ideas off each other on how to make segments fun and creative. We shot segments about the U.S. Open, the royal family, and even ran the risk of spraining our ankles by racing each other through Times Square. A viewer once said, "If I didn't know any better, I would think you two were drunk while doing the news." I'm proud to say that never actually happened. After the show, we definitely threw back some drinks with our team in our office, especially on Friday mornings as a team-building activity, but never during the show.

The chemistry between the two of us was unlike anything I had experienced with a co-anchor, and the same could be said for our friendship. She came up with a signature concept segment for me called "Lifestyles of the Rich...and Kendis" in which I got to travel all around the world giving viewers a glimpse at how the 1 percent of society live. I flew to Dubai in first class on Emirates airline with one of our most creative producer/photographers. I discovered what fueled that creativity and nearly got locked up in a UAE jail as I walked off the plane and discovered a packet of Kiva weed edibles, with the marijuana leaf emblazoned on the package, had been stuffed in my jacket pocket. One of our producers in New York placed it there to give to the producer I was working with in Dubai. I nearly needed a change of boxers when airport security stopped us, inches from making it through customs. Fortunately, they just wanted to check our camera equipment.

That harrowing assignment aside, the lifestyles series was a dream assignment and one of the most popular segments on the show. I shot stories inside mega-mansions in Manhattan, Long Island, and Miami, and I toured private jets and massive boats. I drove a nearly $400,000 Rolls-Royce and ate $10,000 meals. In addition, the executive producers allowed me to pursue passion projects, like when I saw a cute young Latino on Univision one morning when I was studying Spanish and thought, *This kid will be huge*. That sparked a years-long connection with Maluma and his team that allowed me to be the first English-language journalist to introduce the budding superstar to the mainstream. I first met him at a strip mall in Northern Virginia on a Friday night while he performed for a group of fifty people, and some eighteen months later, I was on tour with him shooting behind-the-scenes stories of his first North American stadium tour. It was incredible. I pursued and did a shoot with supermodel Pietro Boselli at a gym in New York. And I started tracking a young Black Formula 1 driver by the name of Lewis Hamilton and got approval from his team to go behind the scenes and have unfettered access to him during one of his Grand Prix races in Montreal.

While the ABC name and our more than one million viewers helped me land these incredible "gets," I was never able to get any of the other shows to put these amazing stories on-air. It wasn't because there was a lack of interest in the subjects or exclusive access, but as I would later learn after leaving ABC, it was because something else was afoot that I had no control over, and it specifically targeted my back.

The Diversity Task Force

In contrast to the sort of glowing on-air welcome I received from *GMA* and the various other shows, my off-air greeting from one of the Black correspondents at *World News Tonight* was, "Welcome to

Mickey's plantation." I asked her, "Do people refer to it as that?" To which she smilingly responded, "You'll find out." Most correspondents had offices on the third floor, and a smaller number were located on the seventh floor of the ABC HQ. That's where my office was located and where I got that cheeky reception on my move-in day. There was an interesting lineup of people assigned to that floor, including Ryan Smith, who was a longtime correspondent and former CNN legal correspondent, and Mara Schiavocampo, a correspondent who had been at NBC for years and primarily covered lifestyle segments in the second hour of *GMA*. There was T. J. Holmes, the smooth-as-silk *GMA* correspondent whom I replaced on the overnights, and Sunny Hostin, who was a cohost of *The View* and ABC legal correspondent, and myself. Five of the network's Black correspondents were the only ones placed on that floor with offices next to each other; we playfully dubbed it "Negro Row."

In the summer of 2016, as the country was grappling with its perennial plague of racial tension—specifically a slew of police-involved deaths of Black men—ABC decided to do a town hall with outgoing president Barack Obama. "The President and the People: A National Conversation" took place in the wake of the horrible ambush killing of five Dallas police officers by a twenty-five-year-old Black man and just days after cops in Baton Rouge brutally shot and killed Alton Sterling in the parking lot of a grocery store, which sparked weeks of protests. ABC quickly formed a team to produce this one-hour-long live special with the first African American president... and had no Black people as part of the producing team for the show.

Negro Row learned of this shocking oversight and put out a group email for the seventh-floor Black news team to assemble. We gathered at a restaurant on the Upper West Side, which was the first time all of us had the chance to be in the same room with each other. It was a much-needed opportunity to vent, support, laugh, and strategize (and drink). The entire group was united in the shock and embarrassment that the network did a special on race relations and didn't have a single Black producer on the team.

In addition, with all due respect to David Muir's bronzing makeup, the only on-air person of color from the company was then ESPN anchor Jemele Hill, who had a brief minute-long speaking role. The only Black ABC News on-air talent was *20/20*'s Deborah Roberts, who appeared in occasional camera shots sitting in the audience like any other member of the town hall, never given an opportunity to speak.

The special's omission of Black personalities was so glaring that Negro Row saw it as a call to arms to force change at the network. If there had been *one* producer of color, or perhaps *senior* producer, then they might have realized the problem and felt empowered to vocalize the wrongs of the optics. The program reflected the power of Muir at the network; he had only a few years earlier inherited the *World News Tonight* crown from Diane Sawyer and remained locked in a battle of egos with George Stephanopoulos as to who was truly the main anchor for the network. This seemed like a showcase of his power—he even got to sit across from the president using *his* preferred "best side" (his preferred camera angle was the right side of his face).

Our crew came up with a plan of action, trying to corral the more than a dozen Black on-air people to join in our effort to get network executives to meet with us to discuss the disappointing number of behind-the-scenes people of color and to hire more. At the time, there was only one Black producer of senior level on any of ABC's eight weekly programs, and that senior producer had been passed over for several promotions and had already put in her notice that she would be departing *GMA*. Robin initially reached out to James Goldston, the president of ABC News, expressing concerns regarding the diversity issue. It was followed up by a sternly worded email drafted by Mara and co-signed by all twelve on-air anchors and correspondents.

"While we recognize our numbers in front of the camera," the letter read, "we are frustrated, demoralized, and angered by the lack of black voices in our newsrooms." We demanded at least one senior producer of color for every show, including *World News Tonight*, which was strikingly missing any form of diversity, and it reflected in its reporting of some issues. We fired this email off to Goldston, to Ben Sherwood, the president of ABC Network, and to Barbara Fedida, the senior vice president, who wielded more power than her already potent title would indicate. She was the puppet master.

Our goal was to encourage the hiring of more Black people to work behind the scenes; we had no interest in promoting our own personal agendas. My next-door neighbor on Negro Row, Mara, and I decided we would take the helm as the main connection between the offices for the network bosses and our would-be rebel group. The thinking was that the schedule for Mara and me allowed us to play secretary for the crew and act as the main liaisons for the bigger-named and busier on-air talent.

In August 2016, we reached out to James's office requesting a meeting, and much to our surprise, he sounded receptive to the idea. We decided to base the timing on Robin's and Michael's calendar. It was ultimately most important that they attend the meeting to add the weight of their reputation, respect, and voice to our unified effort.

In late September 2016, we scheduled our first meeting with James for what he dubbed the "diversity task force." We had decided prior to the meeting that *Nightline* anchor Byron Pitts, whose soft, melodic tone had been a trademark of his decades-long network career, would be our pastoral voice delivering our message. And as a man of God, he had an unusual idea as to how he wanted to initiate the meeting.

We walked into the thirteenth-floor executive conference room looking very much like a united crew with eleven of the twelve on-air correspondents and anchors all in the same room. Steve Osunsami, our Atlanta correspondent, flew up for the occasion, while Pierre Thomas, our Justice Department correspondent, joined us on the phone because of breaking news in Washington, DC. Byron sat at the head of the oversize wooden oval conference room table. To his right sat Robin, followed by Michael, T. J., and correspondent Linsey Davis. I was sandwiched between Mara and James Goldston, whose chief of staff sat in the row of seats behind us along with a junior staff member from the talent development department. Strikingly absent from the meeting was Fedida, the senior vice president of news who was in charge of most hiring for on- and off-air people.

Byron first thanked James and his staff for agreeing to the meeting. "I know there are a million other places you would rather be, so we are grateful for your time and commitment to an open dialogue." James returned the thanks by acknowledging how impressive it was to have all these powerful and important people take time out of their schedules for this meeting. Byron said, "We come in peace and with an open heart, James, and as such if you wouldn't mind, I would love for all of us to hold hands and pray."

"Dear heavenly father," Byron began, "we thank you for allowing us all to gather here on this beautiful day you have made. As we gather here, we ask, Lord, that you will guide us in these discussions, that they may be fruitful and bear favorable results. Dear Lord, we ask that you may watch over us, and allow us to have a healthy discussion without prejudice, but instead with grace, patience, and respect for each other. Thank you Lord, Amen."

While I didn't question Byron's motivation for the prayer, it certainly was a disarming move. "I can honestly say that would be the first time I've ever been part of a meeting that started with a prayer. I quite like it," James bellowed in his strong British accent, seconds after the call for "amen." It set the tone and tenor for that and subsequent meetings. We walked away from that first gathering after an hour-long discussion in which James mostly listened to our grievances and agreed to our lengthy list of demands, including scheduling meetings every three months and the company adopting the NFL's "Rooney rule." That rule stipulates that all NFL teams must interview at least one minority candidate for head coaching positions. In our case, it would mean one Black candidate must be interviewed for every senior producer opening and above. There was also a commitment to hire at least one senior-level producer to every show within a year. The managers seemed committed to this diversity effort, and we felt somewhat hopeful of their desire to make changes.

In January 2017, we had our first follow-up meeting to hear the progress to diversify the behind-the-scenes staffing. It was clear the call to action was not well received. This time, we had Senior Vice President Barbara Fedida in the room with us. Point of reference: At ABC there's only ONE Diane, which was Diane Sawyer, and ONE Barbara, which of course was the icon Barbara Walters (for whom the ABC HQ building is named), so despite her immense power and reach, Barbara Fedida was known by her last name only.

Fedida was a late forties, soft-spoken, diminutive figure with shoulder-length straight black hair that never evolved over the decades. She championed Jewish causes, stories, and correspondents and always put her family, consisting of her beloved elderly mother and three children, first. She was married to a former sportscaster. Fedida would start most one-on-one office conversations discussing either your family and/or hers. It was a beguiling tactic that usually preceded a more brutally raw message about your performance, speaking style, outfit, or hair. She got her start in the business as a secretary in the late '80s and moved her way up, eventually becoming one of the main producers for Peter (another common ABC mononym even years after Jennings's death).

Fedida left ABC for CBS in 2006 in the sort of career catapult few expected, going from producer to vice president of news in charge of talent development. I first became familiar with her at CBS News when she hired me to be a correspondent and fill in as anchor on the weekend morning show. She was fired in 2011 after a short tenure in which she tried to make over several of CBS's signature shows at a network that does not look kindly upon change. She returned to ABC News a few months later, but this time in an even higher position and more powerful role.

Fedida's power extended far beyond her already hefty senior VP title. She was in charge of the network's diversity efforts, as well as hiring all on-air and many off-air talent. She controlled which correspondents did certain segments for all programs and micromanaged the length and style of correspondents' hair and even served as the network's fashion police. Early in my tenure at ABC, I wore jeans on-air and Fedida called me to say, "You're doing television news, not attending a rap concert. Don't ever wear jeans again." She had admonished other White correspondents who wore jeans but usually told them they were not attending a rodeo rather than a rap concert. I was happy to see Fedida join our effort, because I long considered her an ally in the effort to get more Brown and Black people in the network ranks. She was responsible for diversifying the on-air look of the network with more people of color anchoring shows and leading network newscasts. She also created a fellowship program to discover and develop Brown and Black correspondents.

Fedida had been immersed by email in our efforts for diversity in the previous months prior to our second meeting and probably had a good idea of who among us was leading this rebel group. Beyond the prayer that also commenced this meeting, the optimism had long left the conference room. The managers started by updating us on their "progress" and the few Black people they'd interviewed and made offers to, many of whom instead decided to stay with their current networks or weren't interested in joining the network, which Disney acquired in 1996. Fedida said, "There's been quite a bit of blowback from your colleagues about this measure of the 'Rooney rule' and forcing a Black senior candidate on the shows." We thought all our colleagues would see the benefits of having more diverse voices in the newsrooms. She continued, "Almin Karamehmedovic [the longtime executive producer of *World News Tonight*] said there's already a minority on his show team, *him*, because he's Armenian. He doesn't see the need to implement the Rooney rule or have to hire a Black person just because of their color. Minorities are already represented on the program."

You could see the jaws dropping around the room once Fedida unloaded information that she probably regretted saying in an open setting such as this. Her demeanor seemed combative at times. Robin expressed that she was disappointed but unsurprised. She said she had spent years suggesting different names and résumés to several layers of the network, and those people were shunned for various reasons.

James said people that he approached to inform them they would have to interview Black candidates and have them on their team told him outright "no." Robin quickly replied, "I didn't realize that was an option," which garnered a chuckle from our end of the table. We asked if Fedida had identified any candidates for some of the open senior producer roles, and she said she couldn't find any others, to which Robin said she had sent her and her office several candidates.

We left that second meeting with plans to have future meetings in a few months, but with the realization this would be more difficult than many of us had expected. By the third meeting, which Mara largely organized as a liaison between the group and Fedida and James's office, our united group had dwindled among those willing to come in person, with many opting to join by telephone. And once again, the executives repeated the same lines of not being able to secure the correct candidates and how they were working hard to make this their number one priority.

Chasing Pavements

While this was the narrative in the boardroom, something more vindictive appeared to be happening behind the scenes. They quietly informed Mara they would not be renewing her contract, despite her stellar performance. And I took over as the main connection between management and the rabble-rousers. During this period, I started noticing changes to my treatment at the network and performed some research to see if there were some facts to back up the perceived actions toward me from management. In the first two years before our initial diversity gathering in September 2016, I had 212 appearances on *GMA*. In the two years that followed that first meeting, I had only eight. The reduction in my *GMA* reports was incredibly drastic and came out of nowhere. It wasn't for a lack of ambition on my part or pitching story ideas that would normally be *GMA* catnip. In June 2017, I had secured rare and exclusive behind-the-scenes access to then three-time Formula 1 world champion Lewis Hamilton, the first Black athlete to win one, much less multiple, Grand Prix races. I spent months convincing his team to allow me and a crew from *GMA* to go to Montreal to shoot on his jet, in his hotel, and in the paddock on race day. Frustrated with *GMA* not wanting the story, I wasn't even given any reasons why. An executive producer of *Nightline* merely said it wasn't something they could do, but he couldn't pinpoint the reason why.

The following year, 2018, I spent an immense amount of time working the management of up-and-coming Latin superstar Maluma. I sought out and cultivated a relationship with his team and was able to secure an exclusive behind-the-scenes look of his first American arena tour. It was sold out across the country, and our ABC cameras were granted access to him in the New York and

Los Angeles slots. I successfully got our *World News Now* producers to pay for the shoot, and it was expected that this would be a story *GMA* would completely be behind or, if not, *Nightline* would be. We shot the story, and it was incredible. We even got an interview with Ricky Martin, passing the baton to Maluma as the future of Latin music in America. I pitched it to *GMA* and my emails once again went unanswered. This time, even my friend and colleague who was the showrunner for *Nightline* did not respond to me.

During those last two frustrating years, my mental health deteriorated immensely, and my agent and I sent numerous emails and appealed in person for me to be removed from the overnight show because of the impact it was having. Those cries for help were repeatedly ignored by Fedida and James. I recalled how I got on the show in the first place: when T. J.'s health was deteriorating because of the hours, he was off the show within twenty-four hours and given a prime assignment on *GMA*. Nearly three years later, as my health started to deteriorate while working on the show, I wasn't afforded the same luxury.

During that same period, many co-anchors would appear on *World News Now* and ask to come off because of health and various other reasons, and those requests were granted. I stayed on the show despite my diminishing capacities, until I hit my breaking point.

On the Edge

Honestly, I didn't want to jump, but I was bewitched by suicidal ideation. I was enchanted by my death and what would happen after. Would I receive a fancy funeral? Who would speak, cry, or celebrate my death? Would I get more than the usual fifteen-second length of stories whipped around in the back half of *World News Tonight*?

Hours earlier, I had returned from working the overnight shift at ABC News and taken two 10 mg Ambien tablets, with a chaser of two glasses of chardonnay. I stumbled into bed early that morning with the room darkened and the AC unit at full blast, bringing the room temperature low enough even for a hibernating cave bear. I was numb to the touch as I lay in bed, waiting for the pills and potion to kick in. My mental spiral had not happened overnight. For several months, I'd noticed that the pattern repeated itself: home from work, pills and wine, cry myself to sleep (sometimes bawling), wake up four hours later, and proceed through daily life like a zombie still besieged by the drugs and booze, nap, wake up again, and run into work before 11:00 p.m. Rinse and repeat.

The morning of October 12, I cried myself to sleep as the effects of Ambien set in. I was resigned to this being my last day on earth. I felt exhausted, defeated, dejected, and uninspired.

Three hours later I woke up, convinced and confident in my catastrophic fate, which was kind of ironic considering I was awake and alive. I was texting with my friend Robynn Love throughout the ordeal.

At the time, I was dating and living with George Brown, who as I mentioned earlier was my idea of the American dream: a blue-eyed White farm boy from upstate New York. We had met years earlier in Washington during one of my local news roles and had moved to New York City together seven years earlier. That morning, I texted George, who had been working an hour away in Connecticut, to say goodbye. Unbeknownst to me, Robynn had alerted George, who had alerted my co-anchor Diane Macedo and my BFF, longtime FOX 5 New York weatherman Mike Woods, as well as Bryan Keinz, my friend and senior producer from *World News Now*, that someone needed to get over to my apartment as soon as possible.

Each of them expected to encounter a tragedy as they made it to our Upper West Side apartment. I had been within seconds of falling to my death as I sat there on the windowsill, with my legs dangling over the edge. I kept hoping for the impulse to make the leap. Instead, the multiple Ambien and alcohol ended up hitting me hard and slamming me backward onto the hard linoleum kitchen floor behind me. The impact was enough to jolt me into the realization of my sad status, but not sufficient enough to wake me from my drugged and depressive state.

Despite living in New York City, we never locked our doors, as we were completely confident in the security of our building and trusted in the city we loved. Yet, imagine my surprise as I opened my eyes on the kitchen floor and saw Mike Woods looking down at me, saying, "Hey BFF," as we'd referred to each other ever since hitting it off immediately upon our first meeting. "Are you okay?" he asked. I thought, *I'm on my kitchen floor on my back, in my boxers, blurry eyed and numbed to touch. WTF type of dumb ass question is that?* Luckily, I was too numb to vocalize my thoughts, and Mike grabbed my arms and carried me over to the bedroom and tucked me in.

It felt like it was late in the day, but in fact only two hours had transpired since George left for work early in the morning and Mike left his morning show early to come over and care for me. I barely recall that encounter with Mike and certainly don't remember getting back into my bed. Several hours later, I stumbled out of the room, still dazed and depressed, and walked into the living room. Diane, Bryan, George, and Mike were all sitting around together. They had been there for hours, chatting. I had never been part of an intervention, and I was not liking this situation.

"Hey, buddy," Bryan said. "You okay?"

I nodded affirmatively, while thinking, *I am not okay*. I'd shared a lot about my emotional situation with Diane, in our offices and our homes, but I never before saw the look of concern and fear in her face as I noticed in that moment. She looked as if she had rushed over to my place, free of makeup, hair in a ponytail, gray sweats and white T-shirt, protected from the cold only by her oversize winter coat that sat in a bundle next to her on the couch.

Bryan blurted out, "We got you an appointment tomorrow at a therapist. Hope you're good with that, because you're going." Everyone in the group groaned and glared at Bryan, like he had totally screwed up a carefully devised plan of action.

"Sure," I responded in a soft tone of dejection. I knew I needed help. "I'm gonna go back to sleep."

"It's okay," Diane said as she got up and hugged me. "We love you and we know the perfect person to help you."

I slowly walked back into the bedroom with tears filling my eyes and my head down, largely embarrassed by the situation. I could hear George and Mike chastising Bryan for messing up their plan of attack, which I would later learn was intended to be a slow self-acknowledgment that I needed help, and then they would reveal they had already lined up someone for me.

I woke up a few hours later, jumped in the shower, and went in to work. *World News Now* was such a tight-knit family that I felt like I would be letting down the team—and our incredibly loyal viewers—had I not shown up for work. It was a dream job, but at this point, as the longest serving anchor in the show's twenty-five-plus-year history, the role was literally killing me.

Back from the Edge

A mere twenty-four hours had passed since my suicidal ideation and the intervention by my closest friends. There I was, sitting with George in the waiting room for Dr. Ravi Shah, a psychiatrist with offices near Columbus Circle in Manhattan. He was highly recommended through friends of Diane's. George had taken the day off from his job in Connecticut to be there, and I had just left the ABC studios after doing the show.

I'm fairly sure our viewers had no idea something was a little off with me that night. There had been times when I did the show with Ambien still in my system and viewers commented out of concern.

"Are you high?" they asked on Twitter. "Are you having a stroke?" another inquired in a direct message on Instagram because my movements and words were slowed. During a sick spell, I only narrowly missed throwing up on-air and all over my fill-in co-anchor, Adrienne Bankert, before running to a nearby bathroom during a commercial break. I still made it back on-air in time for the next segment. My commitment to the program was strong, despite its spiraling impact on my mind and body.

But it was in that moment at the psychiatrist's office that I realized the true wear and tear this was having on me. Before I could see the doctor, they had me fill out the Hamilton Depression Rating Scale, which gauges whether your depression is mild, moderate, or severe, and gives doctors a sense of how to treat you. There are twenty-one questions that you assign points to. If you're depressed, you give it one point if it's sadness, two if it's weeping, and four if it's severe. Your feelings of suicide, if nonexistent, gets a zero, but if you've attempted suicide, you give it four points. How much sleep you are getting, how much food you are eating, how interested in work you are, your interest in everyday life, your libido—the questions run the gamut. The more extreme the symptoms, the higher the score. A total number between 0 and 7 is considered normal, 8 to 16 means someone is experiencing mild depression, while 17 to 23 indicates moderate cases of depression. If the total score is more than 24, that suggests someone with severe depression. My total was solidly in the danger territory with a tally of 29.

The doctor wanted to see both me and George together at first. We sat down next to each other (on a couch, of course) while this highly acclaimed psychiatrist sat across from us with his legs crossed and a small white legal pad on his lap. He couldn't have been more than thirty-three years old with a fresh fade haircut and the sort of suit that reflected how much he was charging for this fifty-minute session. His tone was very soft as he started the session. "How are you feeling?"

"I've been better, but I'm doing okay," I responded. It wasn't long before he reverted to a condescending tone that I'd come to associate with the psychiatrists I'd met in the past.

"Well, if you were actually doing 'okay,' we wouldn't be here now, would we?" he said in a quiet yet aggressive tone. To which I just raised both my hands as if to suggest, *You got me there, Doc.*

He then asked George how long he'd been noticing the symptoms, which he admitted had been for years. There were weekend nights when I was bawling in the bedroom from being so sad and he was on the couch napping and he would yell, "Cut it out!" George never had a knack for any form of nursing or bedside manner. He described to the doctor the cycle of caffeine to prop myself up for the show at night, followed by half an Ambien at 6:00 a.m., chased with nearly a bottle of wine well before 7:00 a.m., and three hours later, the second half of the Ambien and two more glasses of wine, which would allow me to sleep for another four hours. Sunday through Thursday, this had been the routine for the eighteen months prior to the meltdown that played out on the windowsill.

"Your Hamilton score seems to suggest strong suicidal ideation and possibly a danger to yourself and others," the doctor said, confirming the obvious. He wanted to dive more into my history of depression and what form of treatment I'd had over the years. I recalled how I had mild depression in my late teens and twenties resulting from my childhood trauma and how it manifested itself in panic and anxiety attacks at various points in my career. At ABC, the panic attacks would sometimes appear but in a more mild version as soon as the cameras were on me and usually when I was reporting for the big shows like *GMA* and *World News Tonight*.

"What sort of antidepressants have you used in the past?"

"Mostly Wellbutrin, Prozac briefly, Zoloft, with Zoloft being the only one that seemed to work for my depression."

"Why did you come off it?" he inquired. I answered that I thought it was responsible for the massive panic attacks I was having.

The doctor was a little skeptical of my decision to come off a drug that seemed to be helping me. I've always found that while SSRIs helped in preventing me from getting to the lows of depression, they also did not make me experience exaltation. And all those bottled-up emotions that the drugs helped to tamp down would occasionally burst like a dam in the form of meltdowns that matched some of my lowest lows.

"Have you tried therapy before?" he wondered.

"I have, but it feels like all therapists rip the Band-Aid off on my emotions, exposing it for fifty minutes, and then say, 'Would you look at the time. Go with God, young man.'"

"Interesting," he responded. I was fairly sure he hated me, and this back and forth was starting to appear less than beneficial. At this point, I just wanted him to prescribe a drug that could help me so we could just bounce. He asked about other measures I had taken to cope with the depression, and I admitted to attempting meditation. My ABC colleague Dan Harris had only recently released the bestselling book *10% Happier*, which chronicled his journey as an angry, ambitious young network curmudgeon to being more Zen and a much more pleasant person to be around.

For months, prior to my show, I would head to a specially built meditation room on the thirteenth floor of the network headquarters and sit in silence. I tried Dan's techniques, initially attempting to silence the negative thoughts, then observe them. I didn't feel even 2 percent happier, and the thoughts in my mind just kept reminding me of things I'd much rather be doing than sitting in this warm, IKEA-inspired Buddhist temple.

The last straw came one evening when I was meditating with my eyes closed and heard what sounded like someone sitting down on a nearby beanbag chair. I opened my eyes to see who it was, and there was no one there. I ran out of the room, and when I told our makeup ladies about the experience, they informed me the room had been built in dedication to thirty-one-year-old ABC doctor and reporter Jamie Zimmerman, who had only recently died while on vacation in Hawaii. She was immersed in meditation practice, so they'd built the room in her honor. And with that, I never returned to the meditation room or the practice again.

Dr. Shah didn't react in any way to the story. He promised to prescribe a regimen of Zoloft but first wanted to speak with George alone. I was willing to risk the Zoloft side effects if it meant I'd return from the brink and regain some semblance of happiness.

After ten minutes, George emerged from his one-on-one with Dr. Shah armed with some ominous orders. He was to have the building reinstall child window guards on all six of our apartment windows that looked out to the city, and all the knives and dangerous objects were to be placed out of my reach. He prescribed the Zoloft and even continued to keep my Ambien going and reluctantly approved of me going on an overseas work trip to Singapore the following day. We convinced Dr. Shah it was safe for me to go on the trip since one of my oldest friends ran public relations for the airline and would be on board, as would Kris Van Cleave, a friend and fellow correspondent from CBS News.

The shoot turned out to be one of the best we'd ever done in the three years of the "Lifestyles" series. It was creative, funny, and informative, which is the sweet spot for those types of stories. After three days of work, I stayed behind at a luxury hotel on Sentosa Island, the same property where then president Donald Trump had his first "summit" with his BFF Kim Jong-il. The trip was fuel for my soul. Perhaps it was the change of scenery, the extra sleep I was getting, and/or the Zoloft, but I didn't feel the overwhelming dread and depression I had when I began this trip. I also felt some clarity about my situation with ABC News.

In the years leading up to my meltdown, I had been buckling under the lack of sleep, the pressure to perform at the highest levels set for myself, and the pursuit of recognition by my network bosses. And two weeks prior to my suicidal ideation, I had received death threats from thousands of fans of the famed South Korean boy band BTS, many of them calling me some creative variations on the N-word. They called themselves the "army," and they declared war against me because I had criticized the United Nations for having members of the band speak during a session of the General Assembly among world leaders. It was a brief comment, said on TV in the middle of the night, and in my typical sarcastic jest, but it went viral. They flooded my social media and network email with their racist hate—with some even encouraging me to hang myself.

I'd never been exposed to such vile behavior and lewd comments. I turned off my social media for a week while they calmed down. I was completely overwhelmed by the onslaught of hate and degradation, especially coming at a time when I was at the lowest mental point in my life. I wanted to respond to some of the online bullies encouraging me to kill myself. ("Just wait, your wish will soon come to fruition.") My producers on the overnights were entirely supportive of me and encouraged me to wait out the boy band crisis and continue to do the show. The "army" inundated network bosses and even my co-anchors, calling for my suspension. It never came. I took solace that ABC didn't give in and, as far as I could tell, ignored the calls for my dismissal.

Beyond the silly boy band fandom, I felt the world increasingly closing in on me and sought an exit from the show, but since my contract was only a few months from expiring, the network made an offer they knew I would have to turn down. They would extend my deal by one year but keep me on the overnight show, and offered a mere $10,000 pay raise. My longtime agent with UTA, Jen Campanile, whose own dad died by suicide, encouraged me to walk away. The money was network pittance, and I didn't think it was worth my time and health to sacrifice another year working that difficult schedule. It would be another year and a half before I got confirmation on why they ignored my appeals to come off those hours and offered the insultingly low pay increase. That confirmation would play out in public and garner headlines across the country.

On the Ranch

At the foothills of the Santa Catalina Mountains, located just northeast of Tucson, Arizona, sits a longtime celebrity sanctuary. The Canyon Ranch resort is located a beautiful half hour drive up mountains and into valleys from downtown Tucson. The grounds are beautiful, spread out over 150 acres and featuring miles of hiking trails, desert land, several wellness centers, and more than a hundred stand-alone rooms, or casitas. The tiny houses blend beautifully into the landscape, with most featuring a brown and beige clay exterior and, as Canyon Ranch describes it, a kiss of rose. There are no televisions inside the rooms and no cell phones allowed in the public areas. For decades, this is where celebrities have gone to detox their bodies and cleanse their souls (if they have one). The food supports a healthy lifestyle, with every meal designed to keep you from exceeding an eight-hundred-calorie day, and there's no alcohol, although Diana Ross did famously leave the ranch to patronize a Circle K a mile away and was arrested for drunk driving. The average cost of an overnight stay is around $3,000, but fortunately for me, I had done stories on Canyon Ranch and called in a favor from some friends who did the public relations for the resort.

I arrived at the ranch in December 2019. It had been just over a year since my major mental breakdown and heightened suicidal ideation, but I was still reeling. I was now an anchor at MSNBC doing a weekend afternoon show that focused on all things Donald Trump. The network fed off its viewers' disdain for the then president, and as such, most of my scripts were basically (to borrow a Joe Biden line) a noun, a verb, and Donald Trump. I was exhausted and couldn't have been any less interested in the topic. I was still taking Ambien at least four times a week and drinking a bottle of wine daily. My mood had largely leveled off thanks to Zoloft, but I still experienced severe meltdowns where I could barely leave my bed and would bawl my eyes out for hours. It got so bad at times during that first year at MSNBC, it resulted in me calling out sick from work just hours before showtime, forcing the network to scramble to find a replacement. I was still in rough shape, and after reading about Canyon Ranch, I decided I would take a week off to detox my mind and body and escape the outside world.

Canyon Ranch has an entire wellness center dedicated to sleep, with some of the world's most renowned sleep experts on staff and two in-patient beds to study your sleeping patterns overnight. My initial intention for my stay was to check into the sleep clinic and learn what I needed to once again have a healthy sleeping habit. After four years as an overnight anchor, several of them on Ambien and alcohol, it was now obvious that returning to normal patterns would take more than a year.

Shortly after arriving at the spa, I saw a list of activities taking place during my stay, and one caught my eye: a 12:30 p.m. lecture that sounded like a lighthearted, feel-good topic: "Astrology: Understanding and Preparing for the Upcoming Doomsday Heading Our Way." I wasn't necessarily a believer in the impact the stars have on events that take place here on earth, but I had some time to kill before I could get into my casita. I decided to see two of their astrologers, Jackie and Sean, for separate readings.

I was never a fan of astrology or a believer, but I attended two separate sessions at the ranch that left me shook. There was a consistent alarming thread through both of their readings: the world was going to experience something we had never known, and we were not prepared for it. They continued to lay out the components of the incoming pandemic. They even predicted that President Trump would get very sick from it. I was incredibly shocked—and convinced—by their prophecy.

These lectures were by far the most impactful takeaways for me from my week in Canyon Ranch. I left the resort shaken and inspired to figure out changes I could make for the impending storm. Sean did a personal reading after the group session and encouraged me to get a dog to help me through the rough patches of the next year, and he suggested I drop Zoloft and find enlightenment to a higher degree, although he didn't specify exactly what he meant by that. "It's the key to your happiness," he said, "and based on your energy and zodiac, you're on the cusp of a massive breakthrough." I assumed he was referring to something career related and felt emboldened by his words, while also concerned for mankind.

I immediately returned to New York and started the adoption process for my rescue pup, Tito. Meanwhile, I started looking for signs of the doomsday scenario coming to life. On January 6, I sent my team an email regarding a highly contagious sickness in the middle of China. I titled the email "SARS 2.0" and acknowledged "while there are only two deaths in a country of more than a billion, it's quite possible this could spread quickly, we should do a segment on this." The trip did not give me the sort of soul cleansing and detox I had hoped for, but it gave me a level of awareness about my surroundings and environment that I had not had before.

Back to Belize

The irony is not lost on me that it was in Belize where I truly started my psychedelic journey. While MDMA may have been a game changer in helping me tackle major traumas in my life, I was still battling demons that went beyond my childhood sexual abuse and early adolescent damage. I was grappling with deep depression, a lack of self-worth, sleep issues, alcoholism, and a deep-seated racial reckoning in my core. In the eight weeks between my experience at Canyon Ranch in Tucson and now, a trip back to the motherland, I was able to wean myself off Ambien. It was the first time in nearly five years that I was no longer taking a sedative each night, and it felt amazing. I also felt comfortable in the changes I had made in my life (including a brand-new puppy) to remove myself from Zoloft. My therapist had gone on paternity leave, and I used this as an opportunity to self-diagnose and come off the medication. The sensation of being in a mental cloud preventing me from both dropping into major lows on a daily basis or experiencing any form of elation—a trademark of SSRIs for me—was gone. But I was now left to my own devices, and that meant an overall disconnection from life and general malaise.

I arrived in Belize in early February 2020, just a couple of weeks before COVID became part of the daily conversation. I had encouraged my producers to be on top of the story, and we were doing weekly segments discussing the spread and threat to the American public. I even interviewed Dr. Anthony Fauci on an early Saturday morning and listened as he encouraged us not to wear masks and not to be concerned about the virus, as it had not been declared a pandemic by the World Health Organization.

I was invited to Belize by the government to host a few journalism seminars and conduct lectures all across the country about my journey through television and what the locals could glean from it.

I loved returning to Belize and interacting with those who were in the same industry as me but had never had the sort of core training I was fortunate enough to have received. I usually walked away from those sessions with the frustration of an Alcoholics Anonymous sponsor at a happy hour with a sponsee—they heard me, but they didn't receive anything I had to say. My main message was for them to reduce the amount of gore on their newscasts, because it was believed perpetrators reveled in watching the result of their crimes for all to see on television. It was an exercise in futility. I still hope that by repeating this message over time, perhaps one person will make a change in their coverage.

After three days of seminars and meetings, I decided to take some time to explore parts of my native land that I'd never been to before. I felt a calling to some of the Mayan ruins located deep in the country's mountainous rainforests and just a stone's throw from the border with Guatemala. As Belize City residents, we rarely made it to that part of the country, partly because of a 150-year-old national superstition that Guatemala would invade and take over Belize. Now, as a grown man, I wanted to check it out for myself. I prepared to set out on a solo journey to the mountains and to commune with the Mayan ancestors who roamed this country so long ago.

Just before departing Belize City on the three-hour drive, family friend and local legend Pulu Lightburn stopped by my hotel. Pulu is quite the character and figure. Standing at an impressive six foot four and with long locks, he is central casting for a Rastafarian. Pulu was in his mid- to late-fifties with the deeply ingrained facial wrinkles that attest to a life well lived but also one of stress and anguish. He was a basketball legend in the country, taking the national team to several regional championship showings in the Americas.

My mom had informed Pulu that I would be going to the western part of Belize, because even though I was a grown-ass fortysomething-year-old man who had traveled to more than fifty countries—most of them on my own—she didn't trust me to go alone, so she encouraged Pulu to be my chaperone on this journey.

We left Belize City around sunset in my brother's four-wheel-drive Chevy Suburban that had been driven down from the States some months earlier. I insisted on driving because I wanted to experience doing that in my country. The western highway that flowed out from Belize City to San Ignacio was surprisingly mostly paved, and the only potholes were government-manufactured speed divots and bumps nearly every mile to slow us down. In practice, however, everyone just drives around the bumps and keeps on going at well above the speed limit.

San Ignacio is the second largest city (town really) in the country and home to just under 30,000 people. The colors, cultures, and architecture seemed more reminiscent of a Guatemalan town than a Caribbean nation like Belize. More than eleven hundred years ago, this area was the epicenter of one of the largest Mayan communities in Central America. More than 140,000 people are believed to have lived specifically in the ancient city of Caracol. As a kid in Belize, I had only read articles about the magnificence of the ruins and seen the occasional news stories as archaeologists uncovered some of the estimated 35,000 structures that were a part of the community.

Pulu and I set out just after dawn the following morning for the nearly three-hour drive southeast of San Ignacio to Caracol. After driving twenty of the fifty-four miles, the asphalt suddenly disappeared, exposing the dusty red clay that, with each passing day, was being covered up by the construction crews. It had been a while since I'd driven on a dirt road, and I loved the burst of exhilaration I got from hearing the rubber hitting the surface and the occasional pebble pinging the metal undercarriage. It was quite the adrenaline rush watching the dust cloud grow larger as my speed increased to nearly eighty miles an hour.

"Boy, *big* pothole!"

Pulu tried to alert me about the massive crater in the road that was rapidly approaching the vehicle.

Damn, too late!

Pulu slowly got out to change the flat tire while I stood outside in the scorching February heat looking around at the lush mountains and valleys.

"I got something for you," he said. "I figure since we going to the Mayan ruins, we inhale the fruits of the ancestors."

"What? You know I don't smoke weed," I responded.

"Nah, have you ever had magic mushrooms? It's the fruit of the gods."

He pulled out a small Ziploc bag filled with dried-up multicolored mushrooms. He let the air out of the bag and then pounded it to smithereens. He grabbed the two bottles of orange juice we'd brought from the hotel and poured half the mushrooms into each bottle.

"That's not something for me," I told him.

"Boy, trust me," he said. "This will make this trip that much better. My grandma was a purebred Mayan. We have been using psilocybin as an herb to treat everything you could imagine."

I was quite skeptical but found it intriguing, especially given what I was going through. Pulu had no idea about the personal demons I had been battling increasingly every year since I left Belize as a twelve-year-old. Either it was the Rastafarian in him or some ancestral Mayan intellect, or perhaps it was that massive hit of weed he had just taken, but he appeared clairvoyant in that moment, sensing that I was experiencing challenging times. Whenever my family and I have been to Belize, Pulu's been our most trusted friend, advisor, and, in some ways, handler. And now he was once again unwittingly finding a solution for a problem.

I had only a vague knowledge of mushrooms up to this point. I had heard stories of people having bad trips on them with walls melting and faces contorting while their bodies experienced uncontrollable sensations. For some strange reason I didn't put mushrooms in the same category as the MDMA I'd previously experienced and contemplated as a solution to my issues. But there was something about the convincing sales job Pulu offered about the mushrooms that opened my mind to the idea.

I sat down on the dirt road facing Pulu, grabbed the soil in my hands, and watched the grains of my motherland sift through my fingers while I contemplated this huge decision. Did I want to take a mysterious mental journey with this mystical plant while in the already fucked-up mindset I was in? I wasn't too sure.

"Kendis, the Mayans have been using plants as medicine to treat stuff from heart disease to diabetes, even to get a hard-on. They were the original Pfizer," he laughed, recounting their well-documented use of psychedelics. "They refined everything, including using the toad venom to help out and plenty of magic mushrooms. So going to the ruins and doing this will be perfect."

As we sat there in the vehicle at the side of the road, I grabbed the orange juice that now resembled a muddled cocktail and stared in disgust at the soaked mushroom particles that clung to the side of the bottle. One of other common tales I had heard about mushrooms was they were grown using feces, and given Pulu's casual approach to all things bacteria, I was a bit hesitant.

"Did you grow this yourself?" I asked.

"Naw, from my boy near Euphrates and Albert Street, next to the Chinese store." I nodded my head affirmatively, as if I still remembered streets and locations from more than thirty years ago. And then suddenly, I was overwhelmed and overcome by a sense of just *Fuck it!* and drank myself into uncharted territory. I quickly downed the entire bottle and tapped the plastic so that I could get the remaining fungi at the back. Surprisingly, it tasted simply like orange juice with slimy morsels.

It was so quick that by the time Pulu looked back in my direction with his mouth wide open, it was all gone.

"That was supposed to be for the two of us," he remarked.

I'm screwed!

"I'm kidding. Well, not really. That was for the two of us, but happy you did it. That was about two grams; you got a macrodose on your first time. I was gonna start you off much smaller. It's all right, I have another bag right here. I'll eat that."

I would later learn the general dosage rules of thumb for people taking mushrooms: microdoses, which are around 0.1 to 0.9 grams, are meant to brighten your surroundings and can potentially make even the lamest dad joke incredibly funny as it ever so subtly enhances everyday life; macrodoses, which I had just consumed, are 1.0 to 5.0 grams and have the potential to tap into regions of the brain that can begin to create change. You can begin to see enhanced shapes, colors, mind-bending questions, and find long-sought life solutions on this; and then there are the so-called heroes' doses, which mercifully I did not do on my first try. A heroes' dose is 5 or more grams. Those levels are generally not recommended for recreational use but rather for more therapeutic journeys and can result in life-changing experiences. I'll pass…for now.

As Pulu chowed down on the raw mushrooms, he said, "Get ready, brother, to hear the sights and see the sounds," which sounded scary as hell, but it was too late—the deed was done. The GPS, which was still working despite not having a signal, indicated we had another half hour of road left before we got to the Caracol ruins. Pulu figured it would take a half hour before the mushrooms kicked in, so the timing would be perfect. I jumped behind the wheel but this time added a little caution to the pedal—an accident anywhere between here and the ruins would likely mean a long walk and overnighting in the jungle despite it barely being midday.

Apparently GPS calculates its time estimates based on ideal driving surfaces, because the dirt road we were on was so full of hairpin turns, overgrown foliage, and massive potholes that what was estimated to be a half-hour drive turned into a ninety-minute one. And right on cue, thirty minutes into that ride, the mushrooms began to take effect.

It was a very subtle onset. The glare from the sun started reflecting on parts of the vehicle I didn't even know it was possible to do. The dark dashboard was shining, and who knew it had so many circle patterns that seemed to be pulsing ever so slightly to the Afrobeats playlist blasting in the car?

"You feel it?" Pulu asked.

"Oh yeah, everything is so bright right now." I quickly put my sunglasses on to dim the glare. My ears took on transcendental forms—I heard the tiniest taps of percussion, every string in the songs was as clear as day, and I never knew Afrobeat artists had so many vocal inflections as I now discovered. I detected so many color hues in every direction I looked; trees that before seemed dusty and monotone now had varied shades of green.

"Man, this is beautiful," I couldn't help but remark. But then the fear of God quickly kicked in as the trees that previously made way for the roadway seemed to be collapsing onto the vehicle. The potholes that seemed so manageable even at the slower speeds I had been going were now the size of craters on the moon and at times seemed like a moving target. I slowed the car down, gripped the steering wheel hard, and kept my focus straight ahead while peripherally marveling at all the sights, sounds, and increased smells. My senses were in overdrive.

Finally, there was Caracol—a large Mayan city seemingly sliced out of overgrown jungle. The visitor center's note explained that the name "Caracol," meaning "snail shell" in Spanish, was derived from the spiral-shaped death-defying road that leads to the ruins. (I wish

I had researched that before my lead-footed drive and premature consumption of potent psychedelics!) There were no visitors at the site on this weekday as we walked onto the grounds. The grass was pristinely cut and incredibly green beneath a magnificently blue sky. There were dozens of exquisitely excavated structures at every turn.

Perhaps it was plant medicine, or it could have been the energy flowing through this setting, but I got goose bumps as I walked through looking at these ancient buildings that towered high above the tree line. I felt the forces of my ancestors flowing through my veins; it was remarkable. I realized walking while on mushrooms can be difficult at times—even a ten-yard stroll can feel like you just finished a hundred-yard dash in under ten seconds.

The star attraction at Caracol is the magnificent ruin called Caana (meaning "sky palace"), which rises 141 feet into the air. It remains the tallest man-made structure in the entire country.

As I climbed the temple, I noted that each stair was one-third the height of my body. Even though it felt like a set of track and field hurdles, I had the biggest ear-to-ear smile the whole way up. After fifteen minutes, I made it to the top of the sky palace, while Pulu remained on the ground, lying out on the manicured lawn far below me, smoking yet another blunt. I stood on top of this incredible structure, gazing out as far as the eye could see, far beyond the border between Belize and Guatemala, which has been a source of so much conflict and which had deterred me and my family from ever exploring this part of the country.

There were no lines of demarcation, just trees below me and sky above. I sat down slowly, momentarily overwhelmed and emotional, inhaled deeply, and exhaled with a bright smile. I knew deep in my heart this was exactly where I needed to be and precisely what I should have been doing at that moment. I felt connected to the trees; the stone and stucco that my hands were pressed against felt like a gateway to my soul, sending an electric energy through every morsel of my body. I felt possessed, and also incredibly connected to my roots and my origin story; I had transcended, but to what? I would soon find out.

Things Are Looking Up...Even in Lockdown

I flew back to New York City the following day, still unaware that there had been a prolonged impact on my senses, even though that smile was still present on my face and the feelings attached to it warmed my soul. But I also noted that things were really heating up on the pandemic front, because there were far more people wearing masks on the return flight than on the outbound plane a week earlier.

I had been depressed and despondent in my new job at MSNBC as weekend anchor. I felt my talent was being wasted and that I was once more being marginalized on a dead-end shift. My only weekday responsibilities were to sit in a small, cold studio for several hours a day just in case some of the network's equipment went down during its signature primetime shows.

My first day back in the office, I found myself performing this mundane assignment that for the previous year and a half I had considered the bane of my existence, but now something had fundamentally changed—I was thankful. I was appreciative of this time in the office, to journal, to check emails, and to reconnect with friends. This assignment, which I previously viewed with distaste, now evoked measures of gratitude I had not felt previously in my career.

Days later, New York City was in the throes of a lockdown—businesses shuttered, masks worn, and the relentless soundtrack of ambulances on the way to St. Luke's Hospital nearby heard throughout the city. In late March, I sat by my window and recorded the sound of thirty-three ambulances in one hour en route to the hospital. It was chilling, but I was strangely unstirred.

George and I went for a walk in nearby Riverside Park on a Saturday morning following my newscasts, and as we returned to our apartment building, we heard an awful thud in the courtyard located just ten feet away. Our neighbor from the fourteenth floor, whom we didn't know, had jumped to his death. Our doormen and building staff rushed to the courtyard ahead of us, while others prevented us from seeing the area, which normally would have been visible as we walked into the building.

That night, I relived that moment in my brain, in my heart, and through my senses of sound and sight. I felt some form of depraved elation for my neighbor. It had been only eighteen months since I nearly encountered a similar fate. I had made a long journey since my own thoughts of jumping, and while a lot had changed and I was mentally in a different place, I still felt he had the courage I couldn't muster and wondered if he was in a better place. It was obvious I needed to continue on my journey.

I thought that being an ear witness to this trauma would have had a negative impact on my psyche and emotions, but it didn't. Neither did the macabre siren soundtrack of pandemic New York. My lame-duck job was good. I lost several acquaintances in the early stages of the pandemic but found myself feeling more appreciative of our time together than mournful of their loss. The street and car lights at night carried a glow I had not seen before, and my attention to detail in the simplest things was unbelievable. It was utterly strange. I wasn't on SSRIs, yet the occasional panic attacks that had marred my MSNBC shows by making me seem ill-prepared or unsure of my content had dissipated. The on-air stumbles I would have, even when pronouncing my own name at the top of newscasts, had disappeared. I wondered, *Could all this be a lingering side effect of the mushrooms?* I searched online for the long-lasting impact of psilocybin (the main ingredient in hallucinogenic mushrooms). There were many articles on the promises and perils of using them. But the majority of headlines seemed to confirm my speculation:

> Psychedelic Treatment with Psilocybin Relieves Major Depression, Study Shows.
>
> Can Magic Mushrooms and LSD Treat Depression and Anxiety? Scientists Are Optimistic.
>
> The First Randomized Controlled Trial That Examined Psilocybin Therapy among the General Depression Population, Showing Large Decreases in Depression with About One Half in Remission One Month After Treatment.

I was stunned. Had I inadvertently discovered a solution to my decades-long depression? I asked George if he'd noticed a change in my mood since I returned from Belize.

"Huge! You haven't? Day and night difference. I don't know what or who you did in Belize, but you should do that more often." For George to have noticed such a dramatic shift in my demeanor really drove home for me how unpleasant I must have been to be around. I was a little embarrassed. But for the first time, I thought perhaps I was on to something that might help.

As the city went into lockdown, I couldn't have been happier that I listened to the advice of the Canyon Ranch astrologers and got Tito for companionship. George and I hunkered down like most New Yorkers and didn't leave our home unless it was for work. He was in landscaping, and through some creative legislation, his field was deemed essential and forced him into the office every day. I was one of a handful of anchors mandated to go into the MSNBC studios for our shows, but it did not matter because I saw it as an opportunity to research my newfound fascination with psychedelics.

Everything I found intrigued me. I asked my friends if any of them still had connections for some mushrooms and was shocked by the response: basically everyone did. As the lockdown forced us increasingly indoors, there was a small bubble of friends George and I allowed into our Upper West Side apartment. Within that group were a couple of longtime friends, Drey and Clark, who, as we would soon learn, had the most amazing illegal mushroom connection. They would come to our place on Sundays, wearing masks and latex gloves. We drank, we laughed, and we microdosed mushrooms. It was the happiest of occasions even as the world was falling apart. I legitimately felt that mushrooms were rewiring my brain and allowing me to be happy and whole. I didn't know how, but I was fulfilled.

The Power of Psilocybin

For the moment, I was enjoying the newfound happiness that microdosing mushrooms had brought me. But I was also in disbelief and disappointed by how little was known about the possible mental health benefits of psilocybin. And I was discouraged by how little it was talked about, especially in the Black community, where mental health isn't a frequent subject of discussion.

After so many decades of suffering in silence, I felt not only emboldened to discuss my depression more publicly but also to speak out more about the promise magic mushrooms may present in treating this disease, especially for African Americans. I started diving into books about the subject, including most notably *How to Change Your Mind*, the bestselling book by Michael Pollan, which had been released only two years earlier. The book takes a heavily researched deep dive into the use of psychedelics in the United States and how their suppression in the twentieth century was a terribly shortsighted mistake that may have prevented millions from getting the help they needed.

Yet, as glad as I was to find a mainstream book focused on the benefits of psychedelics, I did not see myself anywhere in its 480 pages. While there were references to elders with immense knowledge of plant medicine, there were few references to the Brown and Black shamans who for generations have lived, breathed, and championed its benefits to their local Indigenous tribes or wandering visitors. I didn't see the inclusion of the Brown and Black individuals in the medical field who are doing the research or who are receiving the therapy for their mental health issues. This is not meant as a criticism of the book but rather as a wake-up call that the stories of Black and Brown people in the context of plant medicine need to be more widely known and included in the literature going forward. We need to hear from the scientists who look and sound like us.

Dr. Stephanie Michael Stewart, whom Dr. McCowan had introduced me to, is, like him, a rock star in the field of psychology. She's a proud product of Spelman College, the all-women's HBCU in Atlanta, Georgia, and there is just something about her aura that exudes warmth and gratitude. In short, she is one of the most magnificent people I've come to know through this journey. Her early life hadn't been easy—she had a Native American and Black mom who died tragically when she was nine years old, and a White dad who committed suicide when she was a young adult. Perhaps because of all the psychic pain she'd experienced in her own life, Stephanie knew from early on that she wanted to be a healer but wasn't sure what form it would take. A Native American elder recognized a healing quality in her, so she went to medical school and focused on psychiatry in order to lean more toward the mind-spirit realm of healing.

Just like William Padilla-Brown, Stephanie's flirtation with magic mushrooms started in her early teenage years—they grew in the wild outside her British Columbia school. "I had been using psychedelics and really felt them as an ally since my mom passed," she said. Her true immersion in the psychedelic world came following her dad's death when Stephanie, who was now a doctor, traveled to northeastern Peru to take part in an ayahuasca ceremony with the Shipibo tribe. She was deep in the rainforest, with no indoor plumbing, limited food and water, no electricity, and cold showers. At night, rats ran freely across the thin yoga-type mat she slept on.

She was in this village for more than a month, speaking with the local shamans and taking part in their ayahuasca ceremonies, during which she was told to set an intention (essentially, what she wanted to get out of the experience). Stephanie wanted to know why her dad, who suffered from PTSD following his military career, opted for suicide. She lay down on a mat after drinking the ayahuasca tea, and as the hallucinogenic effects kicked in, the cacophony of scurrying rats and squeaking, squawking jungle wildlife reached a chaotic crescendo. Suddenly, she mentally ordered the rats to stop running across the top of her hair on the edges of the mat and told the ear-piercing bats to be quiet, and much to her astonishment, they did as she had ordered. "They all realized I had authority and I had boundaries, and I said, 'You can all celebrate with me, but don't come on my mat.'"

From that point on, she seemingly had an out-of-body experience. "It was peak mystical," she said. "I was just like this cosmic intelligence, and was like a god, omnipotent and omnipresent." Then I asked her, "Did you see and communicate with your dad and get the answers you wanted regarding his death?" She said she felt connected with her dad but realized they were on separate paths, and she became at peace with his death for the first time. And it triggered what she felt were more important questions, including, "What's my journey?" The answer led her to the intersection of practicing Western medicine, which she was trained in, and plant healing. She opened a business called Worldwide Wellness that caters to patients in need of healing adventures or telepsychiatry.

More than a decade before COVID, Stephanie was one of the pioneers of telemedicine technology in the mental health space. And with the advancement of laws and her own move to Canada, she was able to incorporate psychedelics into her remote and in-person treatments. She had been more than a decade into her mission of healing people through mind, body, and spirit (plant medicine) by the time I first met her in Atlanta. Stephanie is quite in demand as a speaker and panelist at conferences around the world on the potential of psychedelics—mushrooms in particular—to treat mental health issues.

I asked her how psilocybin, the active ingredient in mushrooms, helped in therapy. She told me, "It's almost like you're seeing the world from a child's mind with psilocybin. Normally as adults, you're operating in a default mode. You don't have to relearn riding a bike every time or relearn your way to work. You know if something falls from the sky it's because of gravity. Our brains are on automation. On mushrooms, there are areas of the brain that physically connect, and lead to insights, and lead to 'wow' self-compassion. It gives you a way to look at difficult situations in your life without being flooded by negative emotions."

She cautioned that not all magic mushrooms are the same, and it's important to know which strain you're going to use to treat what ails you in particular. But once broken down on a molecular level, the active ingredient in magic mushrooms looks strangely like serotonin, the chemical that carries messages from nerve cells to the brain and is responsible for moderating our moods. The lower the serotonin level, the more depressed you may feel. The popular prescription pills like Zoloft (which I was on for years) and Prozac are SSRIs, or selective serotonin reuptake inhibitors, which help to regulate your serotonin level. MDMA increases the amount of serotonin released in the brain, whereas psilocybin releases serotonin in the prefrontal cortex part of the brain, which impacts our perception, moods and cognition.

Stephanie then said something about psychedelics that floored me: "It's the only specialized medicine that exists. It is unique to you. No one else will get out of a plant medicine experience what you're getting, because you're receiving exactly what the plant knows you need." I was taken aback, hearing a professionally trained doctor associate the benefits of plant medicine with such an obscure finding. I wanted to dive into whether it helped with my lifelong battle with depression. "A lot of depression is based on isolation, loneliness, and disconnection," she said, "and psychedelics are connectors by definition, with humanity, the environment, and interpersonally. MRIs of the brain before and after a psilocybin experience show improved connectivity in areas where sadness and depression live in our head. Depression is not so much a disease of chemical imbalance as it is neural circuits in the brain that are not really communicating, and mushrooms help to improve those pathways."

Up to this point, I had only been microdosing mushrooms, with the exception of that surprise amount I consumed on my first opportunity with Pulu in Belize. I wondered if those frequent minor shots of psilocybin worked in rewiring my brain to a point of efficacy. Apparently, the jury is still out; some in the psychiatry field believe they're nothing more than a placebo effect, while Dr. Stewart says there have been tens of thousands of anecdotal stories that suggest otherwise. And while she's happy to be a proponent of something that is helping people, she is cautionary about the recreational use of shrooms. "They need to be used responsibly, because used improperly, they could do more harm than good."

Dr. McGowan also believes it's important to do psychedelics with a therapist or some form of professional guide. There are two major reasons to have a professional along: one, because they can create the proper setting for the mushroom experience, and two, they can provide critical post-experience analysis.

Stephanie encouraged me to continue on my journey, especially since I believed it was impactful in improving my depression and battles with panic attacks. She said recent studies showed that 60 to 75 percent of people had a positive improvement in their moods from psilocybin-assisted therapy, with minimal adverse events, which was 2.5 times greater than talk therapy alone and four times greater than SSRIs alone. I was still hesitant to engage in any form of talk therapy, but she encouraged me to continue my psilocybin regimen, with the mindset of how important the setting is and taking time to decipher the information I got from my microdosing experiences.

But my newfound happiness with psilocybin faced a major challenge in May 2020, reminding me of one of the saddest chapters of my life and ushering me back to that dark place once again.

Charmin Insult

The question from the anchor was fairly simple: "Being here in Belize, perhaps we haven't felt the level of racism that you faced when growing up in the United States. Have you experienced racism there as a Black man?"

It had been ten days since George Floyd was murdered in the streets of Minneapolis, Minnesota, and protests and riots had overtaken many major U.S. cities. I was sitting in my New York City apartment on COVID lockdown when a producer at one of Belize's most popular TV programs reached out for an interview. I had appeared in their studios several times during multiple trips back to Belize, including most recently the visit where I discovered the use of magic mushrooms. Stephanie Daniels wanted me on the following morning's program to discuss the evolving and increasingly deteriorating situation in the United States. I was in my eighteenth month at MSNBC, and they figured a Belizean voice working for a major American television network could add some gravitas to their program. It was near the end of the hour when I was asked that question, and in hindsight, my response was hopelessly naive.

"I don't get a sense of direct racism toward me or that I've seen to my face," I told the viewers. "I've seen it happen to friends and many work colleagues, but it hasn't been one of those things that's been top of mind. It really hasn't impacted me to any degree." But days later, I was suddenly in the middle of a racial scandal involving my former ABC News senior vice president, Barbara Fedida.

On the following Saturday, a week after my interview, I received a direct message in my Twitter inbox from Huffington Post writer Yashar Ali. He asked if he could get my phone number because he wanted to run something by me. I agreed, and I got a call from him later that day.

"Hi, Kendis, it's Yashar. I want to get your reaction to a story I'm writing about Barbara Fedida." He continued: "I have a quote from a meeting in which Barbara said about you that 'ABC spends more on toilet paper than we ever would on him.'"

I didn't know what to make of the comment, and my impulse was to laugh it off. I said, "Well, that's funny, I've never heard that comment, and I guess, yeah, ABC spends a lot on toilet paper, so I consider myself the shit." Yashar went silent for a few seconds and then said he needed to run the article by the lawyers and would be posting it in the next few minutes.

Then a short while later, the texts started coming in from former ABC colleagues; from the Fedida equivalent at NBC, Elena Nachmanoff, whom I'd been trying to get a meeting with for months, to no avail; and from the president of NBC News as well as random people from TV news and friends I had forgotten even had my cell number. Page Six of the *New York Post* somehow got my number, and for the first time in eight months, the *Nightly News* executive producer called and left a message saying they urgently needed me to voice a story for that evening's weekend newscast.

The Fedida comments didn't end with me. Yashar had sourced from thirty-four different people at the network who described her toxic actions behind the scenes and, even worse, cavalier and racially loaded language in an open atmosphere. During contract negotiations with *Good Morning America* star Robin Roberts, in which the co-anchor was asking for more money, Fedida reportedly said Robin had gotten enough and "it was not like the network was asking her to pick cotton." Yashar reported she called the co-host of *The View*, Sunny Hostin, who grew up in the slums of the Bronx, "low rent." Her alleged comments struck at places that were deeply personal and damaging.

I spent most of that Saturday, after adding my voice to that story for *Nightly News*, laughing off the news and the endless attention. I reflected on the years that Fedida actually helped my career, by first giving me a chance at CBS News as a correspondent and anchor and, despite my on-air panic attack, giving me another shot at ABC News and allowing me to anchor one of the most fun, creative shows I've ever been a part of. Fedida released a statement that was timed to coincide with the release of the article that read, "I am proud of my decades of hiring, supporting, and promoting talented journalists of color." Which is true, but the history books are littered with examples of people hiring and, in some cases, forcing people of color into labor, as long as it benefited their bottom line. So, I wondered: Should I suddenly regard these newly reported comments as emerging from a racist person? As Byron Pitts remarked in the days following the revelations, "I cannot say what is in her heart," which is true. But my own truth took hours to reveal itself to me, and it was gut-wrenching. It began when Robin emailed me that day in a form of reassurance: "Thinking of you. Proud of you! Light and love...RR."

Later that evening, I was alone in my apartment when the gravity of Fedida's statement really hit me. I reread Robin's email and began to sob uncontrollably. I felt so gutted and without self-worth and suddenly had a flashback. I realized Fedida was probably why my *GMA* appearances were reduced from two hundred plus in the first two years to just eight in my latter two—payback for my role as a leader in the diversity efforts. I felt I had been marginalized as well when I personally pleaded to be removed from the overnight hours because of my diminishing mental health and was ignored. Their acts and omissions, whether purposely or inadvertently, sent my already vulnerable mental health state into a deep and unrelenting spiral.

I sat in the dark, naked, on the cold tile floor of our bathroom and let out the loudest, most guttural scream I've ever done. It was an evacuation of the dark demons I'd carried and buried inside me for years during my time at ABC, hidden behind my pleasant demeanor and cheerful disposition. I popped a blood vessel in my eye from contracting my facial muscles so tightly as I bawled and rolled into the fetal position at the base of the toilet. My germophobia suddenly didn't matter as my right cheek pressed upon the floor while I cried uncontrollably. Even with my flirtations with suicidal ideation, this was the lowest point in my life.

I eventually stood up and splashed my face with cold water in the sink, and for the first time, I saw myself in the mirror for what I was, or believed I was. I looked at the reflection of a worthless, high on his horse Black man who meant nothing to the television industry, the world, or himself. I yelled at the reflection for several minutes, demeaning myself to the level that felt on par with how I'd been treated by television network executives and how I regarded my worth. Fedida was right—I was nothing more than that piece of shit kid who got dropped out of a window as a child into sludge and had a nasty outhouse for a toilet. That was the reality I observed in the mirror—this poor, pathetic kid from the slums. At that moment I realized my place in this American society; I was just a lowlife nigger.

I crawled into the bedroom and lay down, curled up, hoping the embrace of my own arms would bring me comfort, and bawled myself to sleep. I had been on a regimen of microdosing mushrooms, but I realized that I would need to take an even deeper dive into myself in order to confront and banish the demons that still lurked in the depths of my psyche.

CHAPTER 6

Trip Four: Peru and Ayahuasca

Experiencing your "death" is not like you anticipated it would be, and it certainly wasn't for me. There wasn't a doctor there to declare the time of "death" or someone to check my pulse, no one to deliver last rites. In my early suicidal ideation, I figured I would go out following a bottle of sleeping pills with an alcohol chaser or a dramatic plunge from my twelfth-floor Manhattan apartment building. But now, there I was, experiencing my demise, and with the weird cognizance of my obituary: "Emmy Award–winning journalist Kendis Gibson officially died at 9:30 p.m. central time on August 25."

I was lying in a dark hole on the wooden floor, sprawled across a yoga mat, my head resting on a tiny pillow, deep in the Amazonian jungle in Peru, at least a three-hour boat ride from any other human. I was in a grand room that doubled as a food hall, bar, and church. The metal roof on the building was alive with the sounds of every nocturnal creature slamming into it in a jungle cacophony. Knowing I was at the precipice about to jump into that next phase, the shaman overseeing this jungle séance increasingly chanted a traditional *icaro* like a homing beacon for my soul, ready to exit my body.

I stared at the ceiling and my eyes closed, yet I could see everything around me, including the stars. It was as if someone had peeled back a retractable roof on this giant tin hut. I could see the Big Dipper, the planets, and even occasional shooting stars moving from the right to the left of the Milky Way. And yes, it was the entire Milky Way, unlike I'd ever seen before. So many stars clustered together, forming a dusty cloud in the night sky, and it was almost blindingly bright.

I saw all this with my eyes shut and felt the energy of those heavenly bodies moving through every cell in me. My shaman intensified his rhythmic sounds calling the spirits to release whatever force lay deep within me. The chants intertwined with the colorful images crisscrossing my head. Each inflection in his voice and critical change in his wordless chorus changed the kaleidoscope I observed. My body pulsed and my chest lifted, pulling toward the ceiling with each vocal inflection and rhythmic change. My mouth was wide open, doing the most intensive breathing exercise possible. It was the only thing I had control over at the time. My arms latched onto my side, glued to the hip. Only my hands moved, my palms toward the sky, twitching uncontrollably. In my head, the most unique, frightening, and enthralling experience happened simultaneously.

Keep breathing. We can't do it if you don't breathe.

Why are you so in your head about this? It's a simple process.

Are you just a complete idiot? This is what you wanted, and it is happening. Keep breathing, you lifeless tool.

The voice in my head was a bit of an abrasive, insensitive asshole, so imagine how I felt when I realized that voice was my own consciousness and that I could be a prick sometimes, even to myself.

The shaman came over to my area in the dark and smoked some form of tobacco over my head as I lay there, breathing heavily and experiencing extreme body spasms. I inhaled carefully through my nose and exhaled through my mouth. I lifted my upper torso and sat upright on the mat. I was unaware of my being but still conscious of my actions. Within minutes of sitting upright and my head wobbling aimlessly, a familiar feeling came over my body—I needed to throw up. With my eyes still closed, I felt my way around my space to find this tiny bucket I had already carefully puked into the previous day and picked it up as if it were a holy grail or something deserving of worship. I leaned over and violently heaved into this tiniest of bowls.

Keep breathing, the voice in my head reminded me. Although I felt invincible, it was the only function I needed to maintain throughout. The shaman walked over, stumbling in the dark toward me while singing his rhythmic song. This time, he was equipped with a liquidy substance that smelled similar to witch hazel and rubbed it on my head as I leaned over the bucket.

That's all, said the voice in my head, referring to the puke. As I slowly lay back down on the mat, that harsh, sarcastic voice sounded increasingly condescending.

Are you done now being a wussy? Let go. But let go of what? At this point, I had no control over much of my body. I had no idea what this testosterone-filled voice in my head expected to happen next, but it happened as I lay there, focusing on my breathing. My upper body violently and unexpectedly lifted toward the ceiling. It was in the dark, with only the moon and Milky Way providing lighting to reflect my shadow, but it was sufficient enough for those in the room to say my movements gave the complete impression of Linda Blair's character in *The Exorcist*. My chest lifted my lifeless head upward before flopping it back to the pillow below. With barely enough time to grasp what transpired, I inhaled some air. It happened again, but my body lifted even higher this time. It was as if someone on the ceiling had a string attached to my chest and quickly yanked it upward. My body, at this point, was just a vessel. I had no sensation, despite full awareness of my rapidly twitching hand. Yes, I remembered to breathe.

I blurted out a "wow" while thinking, *This is a powerful drug.* The voice in my head chimed in: *It's not a drug; it's natural life.* Apparently, there were now two voices in my head having a debate. As I lay down on the mat with my eyes still closed and pronounced rhythmic breathing, trying to make something of what happened, I realized I was dead. My soul had left my body. That sarcastic voice that grew increasingly louder was, in fact, my soul, my ego, and I was staring straight at this dark matter. My mind and body had transitioned to the other side, and it was time to figure out what I was doing there in the middle of the jungle of Peru.

The Pessimist

Just a few years before my ayahuasca ceremony, I could barely pronounce it correctly. I first heard of it in my smoke-filled ABC office at 5:00 a.m. on a Friday. I had finished anchoring the overnight newscast at *World News Now* when my friend and producer Bryan, who was there for me in the moments after I flirted with suicide, came over for our usual Friday morning postshow hang. I sat back in my desk chair, listening to Bryan pontificate on a number of topics. Bryan was a six four, blond, blue-eyed hippie spawn. His favorite nouns were "bro" and "meng," as in, "What's up, meng?" That summer Friday, after he'd had three particularly stressful weeks on the show, he mentioned it: "Bro, I'm thinking of doing ayahuasca, the magic drink."

The more he described ayahuasca, the more fearful I became that this hippie-adjacent White man was trying to talk me into a crazy form of obeah (sorcery practiced mainly in the Caribbean). Until this point, I had never heard of ayahuasca, and despite my previous exposure to other forms of hallucinogens, the more I heard about it, the less interest I had.

First, the name sounded like some Ebonics-inspired name for a new baby.

Second, what?

Third, he said, "It makes you connect with the spirit world, your soul, and you can experience your 'death,' meng."

"Why the hell would anybody want to do that?" I asked him.

Big shoulder shrug response.

With dawn breaking through my seventh-floor office window, we settled into this line of conversation even deeper. We had a live Ray Charles album blasting on my record player while Bryan advocated passionately for the plant medicine.

"It's ayawazka, meng," he said in an elongated fashion, probably the result of exhaustion from his sleeplessness at this point.

"Aya, aya, Wichita? Care to elaborate?" I was still confused by all of it.

"Wass ka, washyka, meng." He had no clue. And that was it; that was the extent of the depth of explanation I would get, at least on this day, from a producer going on eighteen hours awake. I was already grappling with my mental health issues and had spent a lifetime fearful of the spirit world. I took this as crazy hippie chatter that I'd never get to experience.

The shaman who conducted my ceremony in Peru told me the ayahuasca plant "draws you when you're ready." He said the spirit often comes to people long before they know or decide they are going to drink ayahuasca in the future. The powerful forces in the universe introduce ayahuasca into the mind and life of those the spirit world knows who need it, and when or perhaps *if* the time is right, it'll manifest. He spoke of it as a living, breathing, thinking thing with telepathic powers of its own. If I had heard this same diatribe years before my ceremony, I would have suspected this shamanic plant man had spent too much time wandering the jungle. In hindsight, I got it.

I met conservationist Paul Rosolie some months earlier during a segment we did about the Amazon forest fires burning out of control. I wanted Paul on my show because he was the preeminent expert on rainforest preservation and had spent decades in the jungle, chronicling his efforts in a 2014 memoir titled *Mother of God: An Extraordinary Journey into the Uncharted Tributaries of the Western Amazon*. Paul knew his shit. Despite being from New Jersey, he was far more familiar with each turn on the Amazon River and its offshoots than exits on the turnpike. He spent months with local tribes, eating their food, learning their customs, and through his organization, Junglekeepers, protecting their lands from illegal poachers and land grabbers.

His appearance on my MSNBC show went very well, and we had him back several more times for various environmental stories. Paul and I struck up a solid friendship, so much so that as COVID ravaged New York City under lockdown, we decided to make a getaway in the Catskill Mountains about ninety minutes north of the Big Apple.

It was the second month of lockdown. I rented a car, grabbed my dog Tito, and headed some two hours north of the city to picturesque Tannersville, New York. This area had one bed-and-breakfast open and one restaurant, and it would generally be quiet even on its busiest day. During COVID, it was crickets. I loved it.

Paul and I met for a hike in the mountains at Kaaterskill Wild Forest, which he described as one of his favorite places to explore. Given all the beautiful locations Paul had seen, that statement came with considerable gravitas. The highlight of the seven-thousand-acre state park was one of America's oldest tourist destinations, the Kaaterskill Falls. It was the perfect setting to decompress from pandemic stress and to have an honest discussion about life.

It was clear from the start that Paul was more jungle boy than Jersey bro, as he wanted to jump into a pool of water that was a twenty- to thirty-foot drop from the cliff edge where we entered the park. I was not one to jump into the unknown, but I agreed to take a video of shirtless Paul as he dove headfirst into this abyss. He was a free spirit who had countless near-death experiences around the world, including being attacked and chased by an elephant in India, and despite his face and body being bruised and bloodied, he credits his escape to a leap of faith into a ravine.

Walking through a forest with Paul is akin to visiting a dog shelter with Cesar Millan, the dog whisperer. Paul doesn't just survey his surroundings; he observes through some super-powered optical lens, pointing out the subtle differences between the yellow and black birch found in the Catskills (besides color differences, black birch is generally smoother, whereas the yellow birch's bark has fine horizontal lines). I was well aware of earmarks for poison ivy but not the bevy of countless other pretty but poisonous plants on the trail.

After a grueling first two hours of hiking at a forty-five-degree grade, we mercifully stopped to grab a bite. As we snacked on a ham sandwich and banana, I opened up to Paul about my mental health history. I told him I had discovered the benefits of doing mushrooms a couple of months earlier but that it was a temporary fix that required regular dosing, depending on my depression. And while suicidal ideation was no longer frequent, I felt there were days I could quickly spiral to those depths.

Paul took a deep breath and sat silent for about ten seconds (which seemed like ten minutes after unloading such a heavy topic to a relative stranger) before looking over at a random tall tree.

"You need to drink the tree," he said.

I was thoroughly confused. "Drink the tree? Not sure I understand."

"Well, not that particular tree." He pointed to the tall oak that gripped his gaze. "Have you heard of ayahuasca?"

Here we go again with this, I thought.

By this point, I had heard some passing mentions of ayahuasca. Still, it was nothing as intensive as my initial briefing from producer

Bryan or hearing the occasional celebrity, like Will Smith, discuss how it made them a better person.

"You've done mushrooms and MDMA before; this is not even in the same world, galaxy, or universe as those. It's an experience on another level."

Once again, I got scared of this sacred plant. But I was slightly more receptive now, perhaps because this tutorial was in the midst of nature, and I wasn't being hot-boxed by weed. For the first time, I was not entirely dismissive of the legendary prowess of this plant medicine.

Paul described a potent brew that gives you superpowers and incredible mental clarity. How the actual ayahuasca is made sounded like a South American jambalaya.

"The main component is the *Banisteriopsis caapi* vine, commonly found in the Amazon."

For the latter half of a two-hour (thankfully) downhill hike, Paul regaled me with his knowledge of ayahuasca and how it could solve many of my problems. He was no medicine man but had been a part of many ceremonies, and as someone with such a deep appreciation and knowledge of the jungle, his recommendation carried a lot of weight for me. I was intrigued.

The Elders

One of the first things you'll discover when googling how taking ayahuasca impacts your bodily functions is that many people tend to shit their pants. Projectile vomiting is also common. After overcoming that shock, I continued my research efforts the evening after I returned from my enlightening hike with Paul. Despite the abundance of information he shared with me about ayahuasca and its powerful healing impact on the mind and soul, he neglected to mention the pooping your pants part of the experience.

Still, I really wanted to know more about ayahuasca and why this particular substance, this ancient plant medicine with the purported ability to heal the most entrenched forms of depression, kept creeping into my consciousness. I had heard of Chelsea Handler's Netflix special and her experience on aya, and I read an article in *Rolling Stone* where Miley Cyrus described it as "definitely one of [her] favorite drugs." While I had minimal experience with MDMA and mushrooms, which had provided life-altering and fun experiences, the idea of trying this high-octane herbal tea didn't sound like a fun time—again, especially the pooping part.

As I continued to research, I learned—to my surprise—that there was a sizable community of African Americans that appreciated aya and its medicinal strengths. This revelation was invigorating, as it was the first I heard that this hippie, White-people-sounding thing was actually something people of color not only embraced but, in many cases, had become leading experts on.

Through my research, I eventually found several people of color and POC organizations dedicated to singing the praises of ayahuasca. I wasn't ready to dive in and schedule my own aya ceremony, but I definitely wanted to know more.

Gabrielle Fouche Williams is an expert in helping people of color heal themselves through the use of sacred earth medicine, shadow and light work, and sound healing. At the time we met, Gabi had been conducting psychedelic journeys, especially ayahuasca ceremonies, for over a decade. If ayahuasca had a Dalai Lama, Gabi would be the perfect candidate. I found out that an Indigenous community in Brazil specifically chose her to become a medicine woman to perform ayahuasca ceremonies in their village, and so I figured that if this tribe, which had been conducting ceremonies for ages, would choose a Black girl from the DC area to do this, she must be legit. And she is.

I was curious as to how she ended up deep in a Brazilian rainforest doing ayahuasca in the first place when the vast majority of the world had never heard of the tea.

"I had a calling," she told me.

Her journey in the psychedelic world started like mine. She experimented with MDMA and mushrooms and found them to be brain-altering, especially MDMA. Gabi lost her mom in a tragic car accident when she was only thirteen, and MDMA helped with her PTSD. After attending Spelman College in Atlanta, Gabi felt a pull to explore the world, and as with many African Americans, Salvador, Brazil, was one of her first stops. Located on the country's northeastern coast, 80 percent of Brazil's Black population is in Salvador. The transatlantic slave trade brought the largest number of Africans outside the continent to Brazil, so it's a place with special meaning for Black Americans. That was the initial draw for Gabi, but it turned out there was a lot more to it than that.

"My soul was calling me there," she said. "I went down there looking for another eye. I went looking for all these things I didn't know I was looking for. But my spirit sought community, ancestral connection, and healing."

The place she found, called Terra Mirim, describes itself in the sort of hippie, earthy, woo-woo language that normally would have turned me away: "Terra Mirim is a place to develop a new consciousness and planetary citizenship for transforming actions in the world in order to promote the balance between human societies and the cosmos." But Gabi put her stamp of approval on it, so I kept an open mind.

During Gabi's initial aya ceremony at Terra Mirim, she told me she had been surrounded by multiethnic Brazilians, mainly mixed race, Indigenous, and Black. "First," Gabi explained, "there are different traditions and different brews with aya. The most common version uses the bark of a tree native to South America called

Psychotria viridis, or *chacruna* in native languages. Then there is the *Banisteriopsis caapi* plant, which is something she and the locals call the 'vine of death.'"

Hearing the ingredients used in this psychedelic tea did very little to settle the lump in my stomach. All the ingredients are boiled down to a brown tea, but the formula is not as simple as it sounds. Depending on the region, tradition, and tribe, there are differences in the texture, the potency, and the dosage. In Brazil, the serving size is normally smaller, like a shot, as opposed to the larger bowl-size portions administered in Peru and Venezuela. Gabi experienced her ceremony in the Brazilian rainforest, inside a traditional circular hut called the maloca. She was surrounded by people dressed in white, with men and women in separate rooms, when she was given her first shot of tea.

She described it as "the most bitter, sour, awful thing I've ever tasted." And then she went on to say, "When the effects of the medicine started to come on, it was very disorienting. I felt the deep heaviness in my body like when you're intoxicated, but it was just like my body felt so heavy and like a pile of goo."

I had practical questions. "If you're so out of it, how do you have control over what and where you take care of the by-product of drinking the tea? Namely the poop and puke."

"You don't!" Gabi said, laughing.

She lost me with that response.

Different tribes have different traditions on how this plays out. In Brazil, the ceremony's actual area is so sacred that any bodily functions must be handled elsewhere. In Gabi's case, a small outhouse was nearby, to where she staggered with the help of some elders who guided her in the dark.

"I was in the outhouse sitting and had just finished, and I looked down at the toilet, and there was nothing there. I just finished shooting my guts out. And there was nothing there."

Gabi thought she was literally and figuratively losing her shit. "Oh my God, I'm going to go crazy forever and lose my mind," she said she remembered thinking. "And after I've lost my mind, I'm going to die here in the jungle. This is crazy. So, I'm looking, and like I look up at the wall, and my shit, it was on the wall."

And with that, I was done—at least mentally. This ayahuasca thing was starting to sound like a form of ancestral waterboarding. But Gabi wasn't done with her story. After the ceremony, she returned to the maloca entirely distraught with the experience, intending to close her eyes, sleep it off, and immediately leave the community the following morning. But then she noticed the music was significantly louder, and the figures in the dark in the maloca looked more pronounced. As soon as she lay back down and closed her eyes, the brew took over.

"I had a vision of all these different religious symbols, raining down from this sky, and understood we all come from the same thing and will return to the same thing. The visions lasted for about a half hour, and finally," she said, "I heard an unknown voice whisper, 'Because your mother died, you will be a healer, and you are doing this healing because your mother died.'"

It was an unexpected revelation that took her days to process. It had been seventeen years since her mom's tragic death, and she felt it had been explained for the first time and had comfort. It was such an epiphany for Gabi, she decided to stay in Brazil even longer. She traveled to different communities, participating in countless ayahuasca ceremonies with different focuses and results.

Finally, she discovered this tiny community in a valley about thirty minutes outside Salvador. After years of being in this community and participating in several ceremonies, she said the medicine, the elders, and the shamans specifically chose to train her to become a medicine woman. It was a long process of finding the ingredients, making the tea, and invoking the proper spiritual intentions. She felt like her very own Daniel *san* from *The Karate Kid*. It was a deep immersion course in medicine and other integrative therapies. The elders chose *her* to organize and perform a ceremony; Gabi planned it all, down to the music and dosage, and it was a success. The shamans emerged from her experience with gratitude, vision, and pride and after several more ceremonies deemed her ready to be a medicine woman.

Hearing her recount her story gave me chills and the impression that I had met someone truly sacred. And I was suddenly intrigued again by something that could erase years of self-condemnation and sorrow.

I wanted to explore the subject further, and a close friend—a pharmacist turned celebrity chef—recommended I speak with someone else for inspiration, a Black man she knew named Undrea Wright. I realized there were many Black women in the plant medicine space, but I was finding few Black men to identify with.

After jumping on the phone with Undrea, who goes by Dre, I learned that Black men played a critical role in the history of ayahuasca. Dre agreed to meet with me to share the tea.

A tall, fellow bald brother who's light-skinned and has a fiery red beard that evokes the Irish-Italian side of his heritage, Dre formed the Ancestor Project believing that "sacred earth medicine is key in liberating all oppressed peoples." He trained for years in the Amazon with several global Indigenous masters. When we met, I mentioned I'd heard a lot about ayahuasca but initially thought it was a White people thing until I learned a lot of Black women were into it. "But I don't see myself in this movement," I told him.

Dre said the tea "is going through a modernization, a.k.a. a whitening," removing the Black founding fathers. Among them was Mestre Irineu, a seven-foot-tall Black man who created Santo Daime, Brazil's oldest ayahuasca religion. Santo Daime combines ayahuasca ceremonies with elements of Christianity, Indigenous practices, and African religions. Dre figured I could draw a lot from Irineu, as he was also born in poverty and faced adversity and inequality in his life, as I had.

While Irineu played a critical role in the modern-day ayahuasca practice performed in more than forty countries, the earliest known use of aya dates back thousands of years in the caves of southwestern Bolivia. There's also evidence of its use from European explorers. When the colonizers arrived in South America in the 1600s and saw people using aya, they described it as "the work of the devil."

The "death" and "rebirth" experience from aya comes largely from the critical chemical in the psychedelic, DMT, which you experience only twice in life: when you're born and when you die. Ayahuasca is the only thing on earth that helps to replicate that same chemical charge. I was fascinated but still didn't know if it was for me. "Ayahuasca is for everybody," Dre informed me, "but not everybody is ayahuasca"—a statement that was equal parts sensible and nonsensical to me.

The Impetus

In early 2022, I moved to my fourteenth television news job in two decades, this time in Miami at the CBS-owned and operated station there. With each work assignment, I envisioned a new beginning, a lasting role, and career growth, yet they were always one contract and done for some reason or another. I always blamed external circumstances and never my psychological battles.

I came to Miami with great fanfare. I had just completed a stint at MSNBC, and this lowly seventh-place station in a market with seven stations was spending big bucks to get me. Gayle King and the entire morning crew did a special video to welcome me, something they had never done before. The *CBS Evening News* anchor, Norah O'Donnell, also made a tribute video and sent well wishes for my success at WFOR. Despite all that anticipation and hype, I sat in the station's makeup room, distraught. My mother was having health issues, a nephew had just been murdered, and here I was, ten minutes before showtime, in tears.

"What have I done?" I kept saying to myself repeatedly. It was 4:20 a.m., and the general manager and news director were in early this Monday to celebrate the launch of this brand-new morning show and their high-priced on-air talent. I plastered on some foundation and powder I had left over from MSNBC and walked into the studio. But the problems were there before kickoff. The weekend before I started the role, my twenty-three-year-old nephew Miles was shot and killed in a New York City club, and weeks later, another family member died suddenly. I needed to get away from the vicious cycle of television news and reset my life. Exactly six months after I walked through the door with much praise, hype, and hope, I walked out on a Friday afternoon, intending never to return to the station. I had planned to tell my agent I wanted to quit not only Miami but television as a whole.

But now what? George and I had just bought a condo and uprooted his life for a third time for me. Our dog also appeared to prefer his Miami life; he'd suddenly lost a nervous limp that only appeared on New York City sidewalks. I needed work, but more importantly, I needed direction. It was my first time in more than twenty years without a job or prospects.

This was one of those moments the shaman was referring to regarding the timing and ayahuasca's laws of attraction when the moment is right. I self-medicated on a moderate dose of mushrooms that Friday night and had the most epic visions as I slept. I woke with incredible clarity and vision—I needed to go to Peru and do ayahuasca. The time had arrived.

I called and left Paul a voicemail: "Hey, remember when we talked about me doing ayahuasca a couple of years ago while hiking in Kaaterskill Park? I have some time off and would like to do it."

His response: "We can make it happen."

Dre maintains one of the biggest mistakes people have with ayahuasca is entering the process in hopes it'll fix specific issues, whether it's depression, PTSD, or anger issues. In this context, Gabi brought up Will Smith. He wrote about tripping on ayahuasca fourteen times, giving him greater enlightenment. "It's very easy to awaken up on the mountain," Gabi said, "and return to the village and still be an asshole," referring to Smith's infamous Oscar slap of comedian Chris Rock. "The key," she continued, "is taking your new spiritual, emotional, and mental health hygiene that aya gives you and looking after that on a day-to-day basis."

The decision on whether and where to do it was behind me; now I needed to figure out who would do it with me. I certainly did not want to go alone and had no intention of joining a group of strangers. I wondered which of my friends would be willing to drop everything and hop on an adventure of a lifetime. Scrolling through my list of Instagram friends, the answer was right before my eyes.

My longtime close friend, Prince Ghuman, had changed his IG name to "Pura Vida," borrowing from the commonly used Costa Rican term for pure/simple life. It's sort of a seize-the-day attitude. Prince is one of my best-looking friends, with chiseled facial features and jet-black hair. We met in San Diego more than a decade ago when we tried to pick up the same girl at a bar. We both ended up dating her and created a lifelong bond. He was born in India but is the type of California surfer bro that displays the "shaka sign" in every one of his photos and everyday life with his "hang loose" attitude. Prince was well versed in psychedelics, having started at an early age on mushrooms before graduating to LSD and MDMA. He always looked for an opportunity to "up" his hallucinogenic game and figured aya would be the next step.

On an August Tuesday morning, I called him out of the blue. "Hey Prince, I'm ready to do ayahuasca in Peru. You down?"

"Fo sho, bro, I'm down. When?"

"Two weeks?"

I still have no idea why I was so determined to make it happen so quickly. Perhaps it was the ayahuasca, but I was on a mission to get it done as soon as possible.

"Say less," Prince quickly responded. "Let's do it."

It was fortunate that Prince's only plan for August was a wedding in Mexico, and he immediately looked at the flights to Peru and said, "Fuck yeah, let's do it."

I called Paul back the next day to line up all the people and parts to make it happen, and within days, I was booking my first flight to Lima, Peru, connecting to the southern Amazonian city of Puerto Maldonado.

The Journey

Angst, apprehension, and anticipation filled my heart as I boarded that flight to Lima for this experience I had heard so much about but never thought I would do. (I was alone; Prince would arrive a few days after me.) It was a quick four-hour flight from Miami to the Peruvian capital and then an even briefer one-hour flight to Puerto Maldonado. As much as I had heard and learned about aya, I was still unaware of its particulars. They call it a drink, but I still thought it was smoked, perhaps snorted, or somehow entered your body by osmosis. I also didn't realize the preparation level that goes into it for several days ahead of the ceremony. Just before takeoff from Miami, Prince called to tell me his friends had warned him he needed to take preparations seriously. Many of his friends had done ayahuasca in the Western way—which likely entailed dozens of people in a converted West Hollywood yoga studio.

Prince planned on arriving in Peru several days after me, so he wanted to give me the heads-up. At least a week before the ceremony, his friends said I should fast, not consume alcohol, and abstain from sex or ejaculation. The regimen is sometimes described as the "ayahuasca diet," and not following it is seen as a hindrance to the experience. But there's little research to back up this practice, and at this point, our ceremony was a week away. There was no way I was capable or willing to do any of those things.

My flight landed in Puerto Maldonado's airport, a single-runway strip surrounded by jungle and reminiscent of Belize's airport circa 1960. Approaching the city, or town, very little civilization was visible. Walking down the stairway from the plane, I was immediately smacked in the face by the scent of the Amazon forest fires. There weren't too many others on the aircraft that Tuesday morning, but it's not like Puerto Maldonado was much of a tourist destination. The city's population was less than a hundred thousand, primarily known as an old gold-mining town. As the entryway to the most untapped portion of the Peruvian Amazon, many loggers shopped in Puerto Maldonado, and many prostitutes, sensing a captive audience, traveled from Lima to the city during the prime logging season.

I arrived in the heart of the forest fire season in August and didn't expect it to be so cold. One of the first stops would be a department store—I soon learned there weren't any, save for relatively small street vendors selling authentic Peruvian woven wool. The temperature in this part of the world varied wildly, somewhere between WTF cold and OMG hot. It was a sunny day, but it was a freezing fifteen-minute ride for me in the back of a rickshaw taxi to town. Paul had told me it shouldn't cost more than fifteen pesos for the ride, and I thought I was negotiating a hard bargain when the taxi driver said it would cost me "*quince pesos*" and I insisted it should be "*cincuenta*." The driver tilted his head slightly to the right, smirked, and said, "Okay, okay," with full knowledge I had confused fifty for fifteen. My bargaining and Spanish-language skills needed refining.

We got to the rustic hotel on the banks of Las Piedras River, a tributary of the Amazon. The wooden huts dotting the cliff of the riverbank resembled Peruvian hobbit houses. The quick realization of my proximity to the jungle hit home on the short walk from the hotel lobby to my room when the desk clerk told me to look up at the rafters, where a massive ten-foot-long boa constrictor was wrapped around the wooden beams. "Ah, hell naw." I walked back in the opposite direction so quickly I left my suitcase behind. "Black folks don't do snakes. Get me one of the other rooms not as rustic with air-conditioning in the next-door tower." It was evident that although I had trekked to the foot of the jungle, I was not truly ready to commune with nature to that degree.

Prince arrived in Puerto Maldonado two days later, just before our major trek into the jungle. Paul had made all the arrangements for us before our arrival. Our guide, Juan, picked us up at the hotel early in the morning to begin what would be quite the hike to our retreat, where the ayahuasca ceremony would take place. Juan would be our lifeline deep in the jungle as the only other person fluent in English and Spanish. He was a mid-forties Peruvian who had spent time abroad in Brazil and briefly in Canada, where he picked up English. As we started our nearly six-hour journey to Lago Soledad resort, Prince asked about my preparation for ayahuasca since everything he had read and heard encouraged abstaining from many of life's vices to get the authentic experience. He didn't have sex, drink alcohol, or consume animal products for much of the last twelve days. I didn't abstain from any of those in the previous twelve hours. I did opt for almond milk instead of skim milk that morning, so perhaps that was a small victory in my preparation.

As our cell phone service bars dwindled to SOS status, our small pickup truck pulled into a small village: Lucerna, Peru. It was our first sight of civilization in more than an hour of this drive, but calling it a town was an exaggeration. The total population was less than fifty people. The only purpose of Lucerna was to service the few retreats and tiny Indigenous communities upriver. We rolled through with the truck rocking side to side from the massive potholes on the dirt road. On each side, tiny, dilapidated wooden houses with tin roofs were kept off the ground by cement blocks. The village may have been the Amazonian gateway for many tourists, yet villagers looked on in amazement as we drove by like a first sighting was happening.

After moving barely two hundred feet, we left the village and landed at the Las Piedras River. There was a small store a few steps away from the boat dock, and Prince and I walked over, hoping to buy some snacks and support the local community. Nothing says foreigners more than two city slickers asking in broken Spanish if they could use a credit card at this grocery store hut in the middle of nowhere. I would have asked if they accepted Apple Pay if my phone was working. We walked down a small embankment to a long, glorified canoe boat rigged with a Briggs & Stratton motor called a *peke peke*, which emitted such copious thick black smoke you'd have mistaken it as the source for the jungle fires. Our team was on board with all our bags, waiting for us. At the far back of the boat was the driver, José, who was also our baggage handler, janitor, building engineer, and sous chef.

Prince and I sat beside each other, and Juan, who spent plenty of time in the United States, sat in front as our only English lifeline for the next few days. He'd done a countless amount of these trips, whether on bird-watching tours or with people partaking in ayahuasca ceremonies. And then there was this stately figure at the front of the boat, Mario, our shaman. He was a sixty-eight-year-old man with wrinkles that spoke volumes of his depth of knowledge and experience, more than his years on earth. He waved and smiled astutely at us and rarely said anything, at least at first, using hand motions and whispers in Spanish to transmit his messages. Mario was a member of the local Indigenous Yine tribe, a group of people dating back centuries that call this portion of Peru and Bolivia home. He'd been a shaman of the Yine people for over twenty years and performed countless ayahuasca ceremonies, yet I would be the first Black man with whom he would conduct it.

We set out on a three-hour, nineteen-mile boat ride up the Las Piedras River that carved a curvy bed through the Amazonian forest. The rainy season is usually December through March in this area, and the water level in parts was barefoot deep, so it took some careful maneuvering to avoid getting stuck on sandbanks. Mario used his arm, gesturing in various directions to guide the driver. He knew the river very well and appeared to be able to see ripples in the water and sand textures the rest of us couldn't. Juan used this part of the journey to play tour guide, pointing out all the wildlife visible along the route.

Farther upriver, in a scene reminiscent of *Jurassic Park*, some of the most colorful birds I'd ever seen, scarlet macaws by the dozens, flew from the thick of the jungle, crossing right above us and flying to the opposite riverbank. If the gay pride flag were a bird, it would be the scarlet macaw. The bright feathers at their head blended perfectly into yellow and green, with a purple-and-blue tinge toward their tail. Their vibrant colors appeared like a kaleidoscope through my binoculars' close-up view. They made a loud bass-filled sound, like the perfect soundtrack to this chapter of my life story.

It finally sunk into me: this was where I needed to be. Whatever strange path I'd taken in my career and life over the decades had brought me to this place. It was the first time I could recall being this disconnected from society and stresses, and I couldn't have been happier. I sat back in my chair, put my sunglasses on, and just relaxed as the cool breeze brushed past my face with a simple smile that remained for the rest of the ride.

We pulled over to the right side of the riverbank precisely three hours after we set out from Lucerna. There were no distinguishing markers to indicate why we were stopping, but this obscure location would be the scene of the most meaningful experience of my life.

The Preshow

With no cell phone service or two-way radio, I was still trying to learn how anyone would have known we had arrived. The engine emitted a massive echo among the trees, but more than a few boats traverse the Piedras daily. Yet, a diminutive figure emerged from the bushes. He ran barefoot down the steep clay embankment, quickly grabbed the rope at the front of the boat, and attached it to a two-foot rock. If they were casting a villain in this story, it would be Santos, the innkeeper at the Lago Soledad retreat. He was five foot four with a hump on his back. His left eye was partially closed, and his right eye was completely bloodshot. His legs were so lotion-deprived, each time he scratched them, which he frequently did, it appeared like white chalk on a dark canvas. He spent up to three and a half weeks at the lodge alone, without electricity or human contact.

Santos quickly situated three suitcases onto his back and somehow climbed that embankment quicker than Prince and I could even in our hiking boots. We followed behind him through a trail for two hundred yards until, with its six individual wooden guest bungalows, the Lago Soledad retreat appeared out of nowhere as the trail ended. On the left stood a more extensive, less maintained cabin that Juan, Mario, José, and Santos would share. Twenty feet farther to the left stood a grand hall shaped like an Amazonian wooden cathedral, with green metal roofs that peaked high into the sky. "That's where the ceremony will be tomorrow night," Juan told me. Off to the left of the grand hall were a kitchen and a tiny bedroom, where Martha, our cook, stayed by herself.

While it was cold in Puerto Maldonado and on the boat ride, the trees that formed a semicircle around Soledad trapped the heat of the day, creating an oppressively humid environment. I walked into my hut with its cathedral metal ceiling and a layer of dead bugs on the wooden floors. The bed had white mosquito netting, and hallelujah, it had an indoor toilet that flushed. The entire retreat ran on gas-fueled generators, and the electricity hours were limited to two hours around lunchtime and two hours at night. That's also the only time the satellite Wi-Fi worked and allowed us to have contact with the outside world.

It was as remote as you could get in the Amazon rainforest and the last stop on the Las Piedras River before encountering an Indigenous tribe classified as uncontacted, located another eight hours farther up the river. Juan told us that less than a decade before our visit, a local Peruvian man found the tribe in southeastern Peru near the riverbanks and took bananas and other fruits for them. They responded by attacking him. He tried to run away, but they shot him in the heart with a bow and arrow, killing him. One of his counterparts across Las Piedras watched in horror as the tribe skinned his body, with his blood left running down the river as a warning for others. I was not going to the retreat grounds to explore.

On our first night, we sat down in the grand hall where the ceremony would take place and spoke with Mario, our shaman, about the experience ahead. Prince mentioned he was nearly two weeks free of alcohol, any form of sex, and meat in his diet, to which Mario responded through Juan's translation, "Why the hell would you ever do that?" Our shaman categorized fasting for weeks and abstaining from vices as Westernized bullshit. Mario said the best practice was to fast at least eight hours before the ceremony, which for us meant from noon the next day to 8:00 p.m. It also meant we could indulge in all the beer we wanted that evening.

The electricity and outside Wi-Fi contact lasted only an hour before the innkeeper turned everything off and sent the entire area into darkness. I initially thought I would panic from the limited connection to the outside world and electrical comforts, but the hesitance went away quickly as I walked outside, looked up at the sky, and saw the Milky Way. It was my second time seeing it, after

Hawaii. I recognized my place in the greater scheme. I felt like a speck of dust in that vast universe. I could feel granular molecules running through my body, and they felt connected to the millions of stars I was watching. Looking at the dusty cluster as it lit up the night sky with its diffuse band of stars, I got goose bumps as tears filled my eyes. It confirmed this was precisely where and what the universe wanted me to be doing at this time. Prince and I hugged each other as we prepared to enter uncharted territory.

On August 25, I woke up with a pit in my stomach. I was drawn to this place and to the events that would take place later that night, but I still had no idea what to expect and was fearful of what I'd heard. How exactly do you experience your "death" and not be scared shitless? What happens if you get stuck in whatever dimension you enter? And what recourse is there if there's a medical situation in this remote location with no outside contact? It made for a restless night. While Prince was on a deeper level of hype for what was to come, I was quiet, introverted, and reserved—traits not generally associated with me. We spent the day trying to commune with nature, or frankly, in search of cooler weather. It was a scorching and muggy day.

Juan encouraged us to visit the nearby tree canopy to relax more. It did the opposite—the tower was a rickety wooden staircase attached by ropes to a strangler fig tree that led to a canopy more than a hundred feet in the air and well above the tree line. This was why they called the Amazon the lungs of the earth. All these carbon-dioxide-inhaling, oxygen-exhaling trees for as far as we could see was a truly awe-inspiring sight, especially combined with the sounds of the rainforest beneath me.

Mario spent the afternoon hunting through the nearby jungle for the perfect pieces of trees to decorate the hall. He handpicked and chopped down the giant branches by himself and, one by one, walked them into the hall. He laid one below each of the yoga mats we would lie on later and positioned three at the front of the hall, with the tallest one towering more than fourteen feet, placed directly behind the wooden throne-like chair from where he would conduct the ceremony. Mario put several other branches outside the hall against the meshed window. It was such an impressive, meticulous display that I wondered about the meanings behind the branches and their placements. "Just decorations," he said, bursting into laughter.

He had spent several days in the buildup to our trip walking into the jungle and personally harvesting the ingredients for the drink. Each shaman has a secret formula they prefer to use for the ceremony. Mario pulled his main element from the *chacruna* plant, which provides powerful psychoactive effects, and some tobacco and Mazzo. The rest, he said, was a tribal secret.

I was filled with angst that afternoon, and the events leading up to my ceremony didn't help. Soledad Lake, it turned out, was filled with piranhas, the freshwater fish native to South American lakes and rivers. The tiny, sharp-toothed fish became the stuff of urban myth, thanks to the 1978 movie about flesh-eating piranhas feasting on the guests at an expensive summer resort. No one had proven otherwise that those fast fish don't eat human flesh, so there was no way I was heading out on a pontoon in search of them. On the other hand, the same adventurous spirit that resulted in Prince going from zero to booking an ayahuasca trip in less than two weeks inspired him to go fishing in the late afternoon.

As the team hit up the lake, I sat back in the bungalow, reading in the muggy heat. I would have killed to wash away the weather depression with some of the beer in the great hall, but I had started my fast; there was no food and nothing to drink until the ceremony.

Several hours passed, and the sun started setting in the jungle. It was incredible how the Amazon came alive after sunset. I'd never heard such various sounds from deep beyond the darkness.

I emerged from my nap in my hut to cries from Martha, who was at the lakeside calling out for the piranha fishing party, which had not returned. I ran to the dock and asked her in my limited Spanish what had happened. The crew of Prince, Juan, Santos, and José was still out in the lake and unaccounted for. I joined Martha in yelling hello and screaming Prince's name. All we could hear was the echo of our voices buttressing against the animal noises of the jungle. Our ceremony was at 8:00 p.m.—only an hour later—and night had fallen. My heart raced, standing there with only Martha and Mario, and having seen this movie so many times, I knew it wasn't hyperbole to conclude that I, as a Black man, would be the first to die. Complicating matters even worse, I was trapped with two people who didn't speak English, and Santos was the only one among us who knew how to crank up the generators and turn on the satellite Wi-Fi or electricity, and as of this moment, he was out on the lake with the crew. "Prince! Juan!" I kept screaming every few seconds into the dark.

Finally, we heard a distinctive human whistle in the distance, unlike the cacophony of jungle animal noises that responded to our previous calls. A few minutes later, we saw a faint cell phone light in the middle of the lake. The boys figured they'd be back before sundown and had not taken a flashlight. Our crew sailed into view with Santos, the person I speculated had taken out the gang, paddling the pontoon into the dock. I gave Prince a big kiss on the cheek, but he and the rest were unaware of the stress my English-challenged band on the pier and I were starting to experience. The team had lost track of time while catching dozens of piranhas. My buddy was so successful in his fishing expedition that the team gave him a new nickname, Piranha Prince. I was relieved for my boy to return, but it had not been the calming experience I wanted before my first ayahuasca ceremony.

The Ceremony

The great hall was lit in its brief electricity break as I walked in about an hour before the ceremony. The crew, excluding Mario, was all seated together, speaking in Spanish, eating the piranhas Prince had caught hours earlier. He wanted to try the fried bony fish, and I had no interest, but we could not eat them because we were on our fast. At a table to the side, Martha had left some dry saltines and almond-covered chocolates for us once our ceremony was done and the fast completed.

As I fired up my cell phone to check in with the world, from the corner of my eye I noticed this tall figure in some unusual garb walking into the grand hall. Mario had ditched his blue jeans and street clothes for a traditional Yine tribal outfit. My heart immediately dropped a beat. His head bandana featured animal skin, with five feathers of different sizes shooting high above the top of his skull. The feather colors resembled those we saw the day before on the macaws. Above his all-black long-sleeved shirt and pants, he wore a long beige sleeveless robe of animal hide. "Shit just got real," Prince said as Mario slowly walked up to us, looked us in the eyes, gave us a long, tight hug, and whispered something in Spanish into my left ear.

What did I get myself into? the internal voice kept repeating, barely drowning out my heightened pounding heartbeat. Mario walked toward the front of the hall, bending over at our mats and placing two small bowls next to them before making his way to his throne. He grabbed a pipe stuffed with tobacco and puffed the smoke in different directions. Within minutes, there was a haze, and the smell of flowery-scented tobacco filled the hall. Prince sat on his mat in a meditative pose doing box-breathing exercises.

I was so nervous. I didn't know what to do with myself, so I decided to commune with the outside world on my phone. I took a photo of the setup and sent it to some friends in the United States. One responded by text: Is that the poop or puke bucket?

Mario placed three soda bottles next to his throne, with the label Inca Kola in blue-and-yellow plastic taped to it. He had replaced the cola with his secret ayahuasca recipe. At that moment, I recalled the less-than-attractive side effects of consuming ayahuasca: puking and shitting your pants.

SERIOUSLY, WHAT DID I GET MYSELF INTO? the voice yelled at me. Puking I could live with; pooping, I could not. So, as any good gay bottom would do, I ran to my room, popped an enema, and ensured that if anything exited my body, it would be through my mouth. I returned to what was now a smoke-filled hall to find Prince in a lotus pose, deep in throws of meditation.

"*Listo?*" Juan asked me.

"Yeah, I'm ready," I nervously responded.

I walked over to my mat, which now had a pillow and a comfortable blanket, as well as a headlamp and a small shot glass placed next to the bucket. I was told to wear comfortable clothing, so I had my favorite long, gray Tom Brady–brand Under Armour sleep pajama pants and a white tank top. Prince lifted from his meditation, approached my mat, kissed me on the forehead, and said, "I love you, bro." He and I sat back in meditative poses and watched Mario shake one of his Inca Kola bottles, slowly get up, and labor barefoot toward us. I grabbed the shot glass and cupped it as he filled it with the ayahuasca serum. After he poured into Prince's glass, Mario sat back on his throne and whispered into his own before lifting it and prompting us as if we were doing tequila shots in a bar.

And with that, it was time. I slowly brought the glass to my lips and consumed my first-ever ayahuasca drink. I never actually tried to imagine what it would taste like, but now I'm pretty sure I know what a liquified taint tastes like.

The lights cut out as soon as the shot was down, sending us into pitch darkness. I lay back, looking out the windows at the trees, listening to the jungle symphony of animals moving around, crawling on the halls and metal roofs, and some flying into the window screen. Mario occasionally sucked on his tobacco pipe and puffed smoke in every direction as we lay in the dark. He had a single candle on his table that he lit, creating this larger-than-life silhouette image of him sitting on his throne with those large branches behind him. There was a specific timing to administering the aya shots; the second shot was given precisely forty minutes later.

At exactly 8:40 p.m., we were given the second shot. And then we waited. My eyes remained wide open while Prince did his box-breathing exercise. And then the *icaros* began, the traditional South American medicine songs used in these ceremonies. Mario blurted a series of never-ending words, singing and whistling. I didn't understand the gravity of his murmuring; I just figured he was trying to pass the time somehow. The *icaros*, however, were an essential part of the ceremony and had been learned and practiced over the years. He whistled when not singing, reminiscent of wind blowing through the forest, or rattled a bunch of dried bundled leaves known as a *chakapa*. These leaves have a specific importance in the ayahuasca ceremony and are said to be comforting and cleansing of the energy around us. Each subsequent drink after the first two is done every twenty minutes. I could hear Mario's feet brushing against the branches on the floor, thinking, *Here we go again.* His small headlamp guided his path toward us as he once again filled our shot glasses.

Immediately after the third shot, our bodies started reacting. Prince got up, turned his headlamp on, and walked to the back of the hall where the next-door bathroom was attached to the building. I was pleased that I had taken the precaution of giving myself an enema beforehand and thus was able to avoid the side effect of the drink. However, it forced me to get up several times to go pee.

I felt the salty saliva in my mouth and sat up. I grabbed the tiny bowl off to my left and started convulsing and dry heaving. Then it was showtime: two back-to-back projectiles of vomit, with some hitting the bottom of the bowl and plastering the floor and tree leaves. I paused while holding the bowl and dry heaved a few more times, spitting into the bowl, anticipating there'd be more, but there wasn't. I lay back down on my pillow, and then the magic began.

I closed my eyes for the first time, and the kaleidoscope of colors and shapes came alive. Beautiful snakes and images danced in my head, similar to my previous psychedelic experiences. The images took my mind through several dimensions all at once. It wasn't as bright as a mushroom high, just colors popping in the foreground with this dark deep-space background. My mouth opened in awe at the ride my mind was taking me on. *What have I done to myself?!* the inner voice recalled, but I brushed it aside, waiting for whatever ayahuasca wanted me to experience.

For the past few days, Prince had discussed his laundry list of intentions of what he wanted to get out of the aya experience. I entered with an open book. I soon heard a voice in the distance, like a child saying, "Hi, Daddy." I looked down toward my chest, with my eyes still closed, and it was Tito. My dog was speaking with me for the first time. I never imagined my little white schnauzer-terrier mixed breed would have this whiny voice, but here it was. Given he was a rescue from Puerto Rico, I figured he'd have a bit of a Bad Bunny accent in English. "Daddy, you need to embrace this experience a little more," Tito continued, looking up at me with his deep-black eyes and jet-black eyelashes I'd spent many days in the makeup room trying to replicate. "*Tranquilo!*" he spoke in Spanish as he tried to calm my breathing, which was getting out of hand.

Mario, who had noticed my reaction to what I was seeing, got up, poured some floral witch hazel oil on my head, and blew some tobacco smoke in my face before returning to his throne and resuming the *icaros*. *Continue to breathe*, the voice in my head said as I cuddled and petted my eleven-pound dog lying on my chest. (As he observed from a nearby chair, Juan told me later that he could see me caressing my left nipple with ultimate care.) The colorful dancing patterns in my head grew in intensity. *Is that the DNA helix?* There were so many variations of designs and colors, but nothing like a mushroom trip. None of this was a happy high for me. "Okay, Daddy, I need to leave you now; you must let go," Tito said, and Mario walked over with a fourth shot as our twenty-minute interval was up. Prince and I sat up and downed this shot. I was so high; my entire body was tingly, and I could feel every ounce of blood flowing through my veins.

I yelled over to Juan, "Do I need to take this? I'm high right now." He laughed. Prince, who has a very high drug tolerance, said he wasn't feeling anything and didn't think it was working. As soon as I lay down after that shot, I was sitting back up and searching for the bowl in the dark.

Mario continued to hum, seemingly louder but realistically at the same levels as before, and I was higher than before. I threw up three more times into that little bowl. My body didn't have much more to give since I had been fasting for more than eight hours, so the next few heaves were dry. Prince got up, stumbled to the toilet again, and gave us the sort of orchestra of the bowels my friends had warned me about in an earlier text. He returned, lay down, quickly sat, and puked his brains out. I'd never experienced this frustration, being so physically close to one of your best friends while they're going through such a visceral experience and being too incapacitated to help. My body was numb from the high, and my mind told my body to move my cheeks, but I had no idea if it happened. Prince dropped back to his mat, and the box breathing he had been doing all night intensified. It was barely ninety minutes since we'd taken our first shot, and I felt like my merry-go-round ride was nearing an end just as he was about to hit hyperspace.

I lay on my side looking at Prince as he lay on his back, his breathing increasingly pronounced, and each exhale a volcanic eruption into the air. Mario's *icaros* got louder, as it was clear Prince was in the beginning stages of something. His eyes remained closed, but he had the biggest smile on his face that I'd ever seen. His hands reached for the sky, trying to touch something, then slammed back down to the mat below. He kept doing that. As someone coming down from a high and relatively sober, it was both fascinating and annoying to watch. Was he laughing? Was he breathing? I couldn't tell, but it seemed like he was experiencing it.

Mario stood up and stomped over to Prince's head. "*Ves a tu madre y a tu hermana?*"

Despite his incapacitation, he was aware enough to respond. "Yes, I do see my mother and sister."

I had given up and resigned myself to the idea that my intense psychedelic experience was all ayahuasca had for me while watching in wonderment as Prince went through this roller-coaster ride. After another forty minutes, his breathing finally calmed down and his hand gestures were reduced to finger tapping. As quickly as it began, he sat up, seemingly out of a trance, and said, "Oh my God! That was the most amazing, intense, and happiest experience. I met my soul. I realized none of what we have matters. Nothing physical, none of my money, none of…"

He continued this post-ayahuasca dissertation for another half hour, describing a triumphant experience filled with rainbows, unicorns, and Kobe Bryant. It couldn't have been more different from my experience. I had a reasonably dark psychedelic ceremony with many colorful patterns and snakes; I hate snakes. What was ayahuasca trying to tell me? Did I travel half a world away into the middle of the jungle to have a mediocre hallucinogenic trip? I was happy for Prince but left the floor that night saddened and hungry.

I got up, still stumbling in the dark from the lingering effects of the drug, and found those crackers and chocolate. Such simple food never tasted so good. I left the great hall with Prince; we hugged each other as we looked up at the Milky Way. It was almost too bright for us to stare at for more than a minute. While mushrooms left me with a recyclable mental feeling and gave a halo-detailed clarity effect to luminescence, ayahuasca gave light-blinding distortion. I could barely look at the Milky Way for more than ten seconds. Prince could scarcely keep quiet about his experience for more than ten seconds. He had a visceral life-changing encounter with the spirit world and his soul. I was envious and exhausted but thought perhaps that was all the ayahuasca wanted to show me.

Spirit World

Mario joined Prince, Juan, and me at breakfast the following morning. I sat across this long table feeling sad and unfulfilled from my experience the night before but was resigned to it being my first and last ayahuasca ceremony. Despite the pitch darkness, Prince wanted to know what Mario may have seen from his vantage point. Juan translated that when Mario walked over to Prince, he saw his mom and sister, both alive, standing by his head, offering support. Prince recalled seeing them as part of his vision and vaguely that Mario had walked over to him. Mario observed a black cloud sitting atop me for the entire ceremony. The combination of the *icaros* and ayahuasca could not get me past that dark energy. He offered the comforting words, "Darkness surrounds me." *Gulp.* At my foot, he saw an older adult, probably my dad, sitting beside me and a younger brother or nephew holding his hand. I'd never told Mario or anyone else involved in this ceremony that my dad died decades ago or that my nephew was recently murdered.

Mario drank the same amount of ayahuasca as the both of us but was such a pro at this, he neither puked nor pooped. His connection with the spirit world via ayahuasca was secondary. He encouraged me to do it one more time. But the last thing I wanted was to see anyone from the spirit world. From early childhood, it was not something I was comfortable with. What if I opened a whole new dimension that I couldn't close and could be haunted for life?

Before leaving for Peru, I had one of the toughest calls with my mom about this. Hortense Gibson was, at the time, a spirited and sharp eighty-five-year-old woman. She birthed seven boys, weathered a decades-long marriage to a philandering Caribbean man, and had the foresight and ambition to pay for a band of shady figures to illegally sneak my oldest brother through the United States's southern border in hopes of a better life.

"Bwoy, yuh dey crazy" was my mom's less than reassuring response. Despite being in the United States for about forty years, her accent remained as thick as ever.

"Yuh nuh forget all the ghost we had in Belize, and yuh gwan do this, yuh dih mess wid dih wrong ting." It was something that remained fresh in my mind.

My earliest memory of my maternal grandmother, Lydia, was as a child of maybe five years old. I had been napping in one of my brother's beds in our home in Belize City when she walked into the room. She was a beautiful, rail-thin, five-foot-three woman with skin so dark, my family used to joke she disappeared at midnight if she stepped outside. She was dressed in an all-white gown, seemingly ready for bed. In Belizean Creole, she said, "Yu di sleep wahn lot dese days, we di go awn?" She inquired why I was sleeping so much.

"Sorry, Granny, I had worms lil earlier franh eating wanh mami," I said, referring to a traditional Belizean fruit.

Granny Liddie advised me, "Jus drink wanh spoonful ah di oil ih wanh help wih di worms." At that point, my mom yelled out from the other room for us to head to dinner.

"Yuh betta hurry up o yu wanh geh in trouble."

I responded, "Yuh right, Granny." I jumped out of the bottom bunk, walked straight past Grandma, who stood there unmoved in her robe, and entered the next-door dining room. It would be years before I learned that the ground-floor room where I was napping had been my granny's bedroom. She passed away three years before I was born. It wasn't my first encounter with the spirit world.

My parents had frequent interactions with ghosts in my childhood home. On several occasions, they looked out their bedroom window at night and saw a woman wearing a long, fluffy white nightgown. She looked like what we called in Belize a *coolie*, a local term for East Indians. My dad first saw her years before my mom spotted her late one night, combing her jet-black hair that extended far below her waist with an expressionless gaze on her face. My parents were way too scared to go outside to investigate why, and, more importantly, how she was able to appear eye level outside their second-floor window.

My grandmother on my father's side had a unique and what I would assume to be terrible curse. She could see and speak with the spirit world. We thought of them as ghosts threatening us, which made her condition particularly frightening as a child. Grandma Nora's home was about an hour's drive southwest of Belize City and meant driving through the country's largest cemetery on the outskirts. Every time we'd pass through that cemetery with Granny Nora would be a traumatizing episode. She would see spirits sitting near graves, smoking, laughing, and crying as real as I appeared to her in the back seat. No one else in the car could see the images she observed. I had mixed feelings about it; if there were people out there, I was intrigued by their existence, but I also didn't want to be frightened by these inexplicable entities around me.

With this historical framework, I told my mom that I would be going to Peru and probably crossing to the other side and connecting with spirits. I was curious, especially from a Caribbean background, since obeah and other forms of religion that draw from African elements are both practiced and feared because of the presumed interaction with the spirit world. I asked Gabi what I should make of this.

"Not a damn thing," she was quick to respond. "People all around the world have their roots in animistic traditions." Meaning the belief that people, places, and objects all possess spiritual elements. "Jesus," she said, "was a shaman. Christianity is filled with miracles. But colonization fought to separate us from our spirituality because it made us powerful."

As Oprah would say, this was one of those "aha moments." It brought me great clarity on what I was doing with ayahuasca. It was not only something I needed to do for myself, but also part of a more extraordinary journey to connect with my ancestors. Dre said, "People of color are already dialed into spiritual and ancestral traditions, which makes us more dialed into the ayahuasca experience." While it was clear Prince was dialed in on that first night, it was obvious I had not surrendered to the experience.

The Rebirth

I recounted my childhood experience and the warning from my mom to Mario and Prince. I was intrigued by the idea of having the real ayahuasca experience and connecting with my soul on another level. Mario walked over to my side of the lunch table, looked into my eyes, put his hands on both temples, and whispered reassurance in Spanish. Juan translated, "He has done countless ceremonies, and everyone who has crossed over has returned. The spirits you'll encounter will not be scary and will wrap you with their love from that moment and for years."

Prince pulled me aside to assure me this would be the best decision I'd ever make if I went through with the second round. "It is a thousand percent a positive experience. I left there so happy and got so much clarity about who we are, the meaning of life, and what happens after we die. I connected with Kobe Bryant last night." Prince always had a borderline psychotic obsession with Kobe, so if Mamba made it to his ceremony, it must have been an orgasmic experience.

I retreated to my bungalow, lying in bed as the day's heat and lack of air-conditioning transformed the room into a sweltering sauna. My mind still needed to be made up on round two, but I adhered to the rules of the fast and made sure my beer consumption took place before noon. We were limited to a vegetarian diet when we weren't fasting, so I just stuck with that plan.

Eventually, I passed out in the heat and slipped into one of the most vivid and memorable dreams ever. I was riding my bike as a child in this colorful Belizean neighborhood. My mom and brothers were running behind me, ready to catch me if I fell. I got to a street corner, and a bright blue-and-green house with the most colorful flowers was on display. Standing in that front yard and smiling was a much younger version of my dad, the type I only recalled from old photos of him with a full Afro and a good hundred pounds less than his frame for much of my time with him. His grin was from ear to ear as I rode along on that bike, leaving him behind while my living family members continued running and cheering me on.

I woke up in a cold sweat, partly because it was Africa hot inside that room, but also from the chilling nature of the dream. Perhaps it was the lingering effects of the ayahuasca from last night, or perhaps it was my calling. That internal question of *What did I get myself into?* was never answered. For the previous twelve hours, Prince had been running around regaling us with the happiest of experiences he had bonding with his inner soul. My only takeaway was a creepy conversation with my three-year-old dog. There was no way I could leave here without getting the answers to why I was on this journey in the first place.

I consciously tried to be more present ahead of the ceremony that night. Instead of connecting to the outside world, I sat on my mat an hour before the start time in the meditation poses, doing box breathing: inhale for four seconds, hold for four seconds, and exhale for four seconds. It was a technique I had learned from a talent coach and therapist to reduce anxiety and stress. That night, I used it to take me to another dimension. Mario said we would likely not puke or shit as much as we did during the first ceremony. Generally, your first ayahuasca session cleanses your mind and body of toxins and demons; the recommended second ceremony is when you can connect with your purpose.

We resumed the ritual of the previous night. Mario with a deep hug to both of us, me and Prince kissing each other and admitting our mutual love, and then on the mat, holding that shot glass with great reverence after Mario had delivered the first dose. Mario told us to ask the tea to "take us to another dimension," which garnered a *gulp* from the internal. I did, and it was off to the races. This time, I closed my eyes and concentrated on those box-breathing exercises from the start.

No matter how many medicine people or experts you speak with, how much literature you read, or how many documentaries you watch, nothing prepares you for ayahuasca. Each experience will be different and uniquely your own. I've long heard about the active ingredient in ayahuasca, telepathine, which is often called *telepatía* because of the perceived superpowers it gives you. That second night, I finally understood what that all meant.

Unlike night one, where my eyes remained open, expecting to watch the spirits as they came in from the edges of the jungle, I was inside my mind. Mario remained quiet throughout the first two rounds of shots, opting to softly begin the *icaros* nearly an hour into the session. Prince and I were also very quiet; instead of the occasional banter, we concentrated on breathing. That second shot had differing effects on us—it sent me to the bathroom for one of my seven pee breaks that night, followed by Prince's now familiar orchestral bowel performance, and another twenty minutes passed before Mario lit his tiny candle posted to the right of his throne and grabbed his Inca Kola bottle for round number three. I wondered how Mario—who was doing two shots for every one he gave us—didn't throw up. Gabi would later tell me her shamans taught her to drink beforehand, and if it needed to exit her body, they did that outside the hall before anyone could see it. Who knew the medicine people also practiced a bit of deception?

The night before, I was lying on my back with my arms folded, but for this second ceremony, I had a more open posture. My breathing was concentrated, and both arms were beside me, my palms facing the sky. The first reaction I had to the drink was my perception of sound. Most nights the jungle noises were intense, but I felt like I had sonar abilities. I could hear every animal interacting with the hall outside and inside. There was a bat we noticed before the lights went out for the night, and frequently as I lay back on my mat, I could hear the high-pitched squeaks and fluttering wings, at times a little too close to my ears for comfort. Normally I would be freaked out by that sort of interaction with a bat, but I was strangely calm. The *icaros* kicked in after that second shot, this time with a higher pitch, only because I was starting to feel the effects of the aya.

Keep breathing. Reflect defeat or resignation that there is no turning back from where we are.

Breaking the seal during a hallucinogenic trip is probably not the best idea. I grabbed the headlamp and stumbled around the corner to the outside toilet. It was apparent how wobbly I had become, and we were only forty minutes into this ceremony. Then, I broke my rule when doing any hallucinogenic drug and looked at myself in the mirror as I washed my hands.

Not a good idea!

Concentrate on breathing! Inhale for four seconds, hold for four seconds, exhale four, and hold four.

With each breath, my body sank deeper into the mat while my mind felt lighter and lighter. The visuals of the night before weren't there, at least not yet. I was staring at dark matter, no snakes, no helix, no Tito. My hands remained near my waist, palms upright. My fingers twitched. My brain directed my hands to stay in that position, but my body fought that force, shaking my hands uncontrollably. I had no control over them but was well aware of the movement.

We can't do this unless you remember to breathe.

That reminder from the internal voice sounded different this time. My breathing synced with the different pitches of Mario's *icaros*. Then, I saw the Milky Way. It wasn't the dusty version I saw the night before when I was still rolling but a clear, crisp, detailed image of our galaxy. I looked to the outer edges of my view, where the stars trailed off a bit, and observed every detail of the cosmic dust. I was looking through the roof, but my eyes remained closed. It made me smile to think that I could see through the walls. I focused my attention to the right of the hall and peered outside; I saw the satellite dish and the bird feeder that attracted an array of vocal birds.

Look back at the stars.

I followed the internal's directions, and the Milky Way had changed. I had traveled to another dimension of the universe. With my eyes closed and my body firmly pressed against the mat, I traveled outside the hall. Within seconds, I was flying over the darkened

Amazon rainforest. I saw some of the many fires, then flew over the coastal city of Lima on the Pacific, crossed over the mountains outside Bogotá and Cartagena, illuminated by soft street lighting, and glided over the dark Caribbean Sea. It was interesting to note the jungle and ocean appeared the same at night, awash in pure darkness. I approached the Miami area from the southeastern side, which I'd done many times. The multicolor lights that bathed the art deco buildings on Ocean Drive had a scope that reached well into the night sky. Just a few blocks to the west, I arrived at my South Beach condo and flew into my second-floor window. It didn't matter that our hurricane-force windows were closed; I penetrated everything. I flew through the bedroom and hovered in the living room and saw Tito and George sitting on the couch next to each other, watching television. Tito looked up, knowing I was present; his nose twitched as if he smelled something familiar.

Yo, you need to piss again. Let's go!

That internal voice, becoming increasingly unrecognizable, snapped me out of my telepathic journey and returned me to the mat just in time as I had to piss. I felt around for the lamp but realized I didn't need it. I could see the back of my hand, even in the dark, with my eyes closed. I could see the empty dark blue puke bowl and knew I had powers that could see through my eyelids and pierce the darkness.

It's okay; I'll be here when you return.

I slowly stood and looked toward Mario at the front of the room, who was smoking that pipe in the dark. I turned around to make sure I really could see in the night; I could. My right foot extended an exaggerated step over the pillow at the top of my mat, followed deliberately by my left foot. I put my hands out as a precaution, but there was no reason for it; I could see clearly what was ahead. I was still shaky from the aya but went to the great hall door and walked outside to the toilet. My eyes remained closed during the whole experience. As I returned to the mat, Mario approached us with his third shot of ayahuasca. I sat upright on the mat and expressed my intentions again: to be transported to another dimension. I lay back on that pillow and never felt so happy to be anywhere in my life. I could see through objects and saw my dog and my man. This was already a fantastic experience. I got utterly lost in the moment. It was as if my body did not belong to me anymore.

Yo, you forgot to breathe. While you may feel like you're omnipotent, there's only so much you can...we can do without the breath.

The tone and use of "we" from my internal voice struck me like I wasn't alone, and the voice in my head had a slightly different personality. Then it hit, and I had to puke. I sat up and felt around for the bowl. The first few heaves were all dry. But the fourth felt powerful, with the substance coming deep from the bottom of my empty stomach, with its acid burning my esophagus as it pushed through. My mouth opened wide by this point, accustomed to the routine, and into the bowl shot barely a piddle of spit. As quickly as I lay back down, my stomach was ready for war, and it bolted me back up to the sitting position as I hurled the beer, the vegetarian breakfast, lunch, and finally, what was the magic elixir. Ayahuasca is the only thing I've ever had that tastes the same going down as it does while throwing it up. Mario stumbled over, bent over near my face, which was buried down into the bowl, and smoked three more puffs of the tobacco. He then poured a little witch hazel into his hand and rubbed it over my head.

I slowly lay back on my mat, and then the magic began. The snakes and helix that danced through my brain the night before were gone. I was staring deep into a black hole. As I traveled through wormholes, circular purple streaks wrapped around my vision and stretched the faster I moved. My mouth opened as I marveled at the visuals. It was fascinating but not the "thousand percent happy" experience Prince had promised. I tried forcing myself to smile to avoid my brain entering hostile territory—the colors and lights were in sync with the *icaros*. The music was creating trails in my brain. The *icaros* were this homing beacon for the images in my head, drawn to the tunes of this Peruvian Pied Piper.

Breathe.

I inhaled the deepest breath, even though I had no control over any part of my body. Long gone was the box breathing; my mouth was wide open, and my body had become a vessel. The only thing I could do was tell myself to breathe. Mario sensed something and increased the pitch and tempo of the *icaros*. Then it happened. My chest rapidly and violently lifted, bringing my entire upper torso with it toward the sky before slamming me back down to the mat. And again. This time, the force pulled me even higher into the air. It felt like someone had attached suction to my chest and pulled it toward the ceiling. That second jolt lifted two-thirds of my body upward and flopped it back down aggressively. Once back down on the mat, the visuals were gone, but I stared at this dark mass that felt strangely familiar. I knew I was breathing, but I no longer had control over that or any aspect of my body. I was focused solely on this dark matter.

"I gotta say you are one fine vessel…thank you for maintaining such a fine ass."

Besides being incredibly cocky, my internal voice no longer sounded internal. It was now coming directly from the dark matter in front of me.

"Wait, are you…me?"

"I am, and you are my body."

"Do you have a name? Nice to meet you."

"I don't have a name. Nice to meet you; let's shake hands."

I mentally reached out to shake its hand. "Psych! I don't have hands, dumbass."

My eyes remained closed as I realized I was staring at my soul. Those two powerful physical reactions I had a few seconds earlier were my soul leaving my earthly vessel. The *icaros* facilitated its aggressive exit from my body.

"Wow, you're my soul! Does that mean we're like soul brothers or soul sisters?"

"Knowing you, we're more like soul sisters."

"You mean like, hey sista, soul sista?" We broke into a song in unison. "Hey sista go sista, soul sista flow sista." We went into a mental dance together as we continued with the first few "soul sista" bars of "Lady Marmalade."

You are me, wow, I thought while mentally smiling. It was the first time I'd felt any happiness in this ceremony. It would not stay that way for very long. I had so many questions I wanted to be answered.

"First, do I refer to you as he, she, they? What's your pronoun?" I couldn't see, but I could feel an eye roll from my soul at that question.

"Where will my next job be?"

"Am I in the right relationship?"

"How are my dad and Myles doing in the afterlife?"

My soul didn't respond to the barrage of questions. Instead, we went flying through whatever dimension we were occupying. As we streaked through space like Starfleet officers in warp drive, the colors stayed in the purple-and-black spectrum. Every time we stopped moving, I would try to ask a question, and my soul wouldn't respond but would take us on another psychedelic ride through the time-space continuum.

"I know you've been on endless diets," it said, "but thank you for providing me with a beautiful body to occupy."

"It hasn't been easy."

"I know, especially with the amount of alcohol you drink."

"I thought this was supposed to be a positive experience, not another judgmental therapy session."

"You're not capable of having a positive experience. You're constantly looking for how life will go south for you, and when it does, you say, 'I knew it.'"

I'd heard the same thing from therapists, but it hit deeper when it came from your soul.

"You don't know how to love yourself; in fact, you don't love yourself. You don't love me! You do know us souls have feelings too?"

"You do?"

"Naw, just kidding." My soul was a smug, sarcastic, narcissistic prick. In other words, it was me.

"But you really have to learn to nurture your soul. You flew home to watch Tito and George, to check on your so-called loved ones, but no one will love you as much as you love yourself. And for the past forty-plus years, you've been in a loveless relationship with yourself."

Well, this is taking a dark turn, I thought. My soul continued, "It is why you've thought about killing yourself so many times; it is why you find elation in suicidal ideation. Because you do not love yourself." He/she/it wasn't wrong.

"When's the last time you said you loved yourself?" I couldn't recall a single time. "You have such a beautiful soul; I'm fairly nice, if I say so myself. What's not to love?"

I had so much warmth for this dark matter taking me to church that I said mentally, "I love you!"

"Repeat it, and say it often. I want you to start every day by looking at yourself in the mirror, looking into your soul, and saying, 'I love you!' Do it for me right now."

I whispered, "I love you."

"Repeat it, and louder!"

I finally was given some control of a part of my body and moved my lips quietly, saying, "I love you."

"Again!"

Slightly louder, I said, "I love you."

"Again, so that they can hear you."

"I love you!" I repeated at the top of my lungs, "I LOVE YOU!"

"How did that feel?"

I had never felt so much love for anyone, particularly myself.

"Thank you," it said. "Please start each day loving yourself and being thankful for this amazing life. I don't have a horse in this race; if you successfully killed yourself, I would move on to another vessel. But I love you and want us to have a long life together."

I said again, "I love you!" I suddenly regained control of my arms and stretched them out to hug my soul.

"Okay, let me back in."

At that point, my mouth opened as if I was yawning, but it was the widest I'd ever opened my mouth before. My eyes remained closed as that dark matter I had been speaking with turned into a massive white orb. It slowly flew into my gaping mouth. I felt a gush of warmth as it moved down my throat and into my stomach. That warm light burst into a million different pieces and returned to all parts of my corpse. My soul had returned home. The voice didn't go away but returned to more of an internal tone. "You'll be fine," it reassured me.

"Wow!" I said out loud. I didn't expect that. "Holy shit, wow!" I sat up and wrapped my body with my arms so tightly, as I was trying to hug my inner soul. I kept holding myself tight for several minutes, and despite the reassurance from my inside voice that it was okay, I was guilty. My soul was beautiful. Why would I have wanted to separate myself from that? How had I not loved myself all these years? I rocked my body back and forth while hugging myself and crying quietly. What started as some sniffles and tears soon turned into full-blown bawling. I'd never bawled in such an uncontrollable manner, wildly, erratically, and ultimately cathartically. As I wept, I repeatedly said, "I'm so sorry!" I apologized to my soul for not loving myself more all these decades. I couldn't stop feeling sorry for my soul.

After several minutes, Mario walked over, poured more witch hazel on my head, and hugged me. It was the comfort I needed at that moment. It also made me situationally aware again. I kept rocking as I slowly stopped crying and opened my eyes. Mario had lit the candle, illuminating his throne and branches once more. I looked over at Prince, lying down with his hands again in the air reaching for the stars. I looked at Mario and said, "Wow, I didn't expect that. Holy shit." Only two hours had passed, and the ayahuasca still flowed through my veins, but I felt fulfilled. Whatever I was going to get out of this experience, I had already accomplished and received my marching orders, and it was time to act on it.

"Mario, *termine. Listo a dormir.*" I told him in slightly poor Spanish that I was finished and ready to sleep. He walked over to me, poured more witch hazel on my head, and cupped my head as he performed some prayerful chant. I slowly stood, and Mario gave me a deep hug connecting through my bones and into my soul. "Thank you, Mario, Juan. *Buenas noches.*"

I walked to the back of the hall, but this time with my headlamp. The superpowers that allowed me to see in the dark and through objects were gone. But it was apparent ayahuasca's hallucinogenic effects were still there. I could hear the animals walking, flying, and slithering deep beyond the forest line. The stardust of the Milky Way was brighter and clearer than my first ceremony, and I felt connected with every entity in the universe. I just knew some identical particles comprising those celestial bodies were running through my body. It was surreal. I was not ready for bed, but I no longer needed to be in that hall. I delicately grabbed the side rail of the stairs leading to my hut and gently walked up, still dizzy and shaky.

My intention had been to enter another dimension, and that was certainly achieved. I expected to have all my questions answered by the end of the experience, but I realized none of it mattered. I'd never felt love for myself as I did when I lay in bed beneath that white mosquito netting. And there was a different sort of love I felt in that room. I looked around, and while I couldn't see them, I could feel the energy of my dad, my nephew, and my grandmothers. I was taught from an early age to fear the spirit world, but I felt surrounded by their warmth and love. Now that I had crossed over to the spirit world and visited George and Tito while in that dimension, I realized those childhood hauntings were just the spirit world communicating with me. There was nothing scary for me anymore about that world. As Mario said, the spirit world wrapped me in their love, and I eventually trailed off to sleep.

A New Dawn

Everyone should experience waking up in a jungle. Hollywood's most talented sound effects artist couldn't replicate the different audio vibrations that early morning. The colors of a jungle sunrise are the deepest yellows and reds you'll ever see, though it could also have been the lingering effects of the ayahuasca. I hadn't been up for sunrise this trip but was excited to be alive and greet this new life.

First, I couldn't wait to look at myself in the mirror and shout, "I love you!" Next, I left my bungalow, walked a hundred yards into the jungle in the predawn darkness, and did the delicate climb up into the tree canopy. Nightfall was still at the base as I set out to scale the rickety structure.

By the time I climbed more than a hundred feet in the air, I had stepped into the light and started a new life. I looked out as the sun rose above the horizon on that chilly morning, basking in the warm rays, listening to the jungle sounds, and marveling at the rosy hues. It wasn't just the start of a new day; August 26 was the first day I felt alive. I knew from that moment with the ultimate confidence that no matter what happened, I could handle it. At that moment, with the sun's rays warming my skin, I felt connected with the universe. The weight I'd carried a lifetime, embarrassed by my impoverished childhood, had lifted. I realized through this journey that my escape from poverty was a badge of honor and not something to be ashamed of. And most importantly, my heart was bursting with self-love. I was never happier to be alive and to be myself.

CHAPTER 7

Trip Five: Psilocybin and Dr. Scott-Ward

I first became aware of Dr. Gillian Scott-Ward, a clinically licensed psychologist and filmmaker, during the pandemic when a friend sent a copy of the highly acclaimed documentary short called *Back to Natural*. The sixty-nine-minute film chronicled the roots of Black people's struggles with our natural hair. There was a particular quote from Malcolm X featured in the documentary that struck me to the point that I wrote it down: "I do think that you'll find that Black people in America as they strive to throw off the shackles of mental colonialism will also probably reflect an effort to show…to throw off the shackles of cultural colonialism and they may begin to reflect the desires of the room with the standards of their own."

I had no idea what it was about that quote that triggered me or why I had the impulse to record it. Over the years, and as I went about writing this book, I connected with a friend in Spain who happened to have been featured in Dr. Scott-Ward's hair documentary. She said, "The more I hear about your book, the more I think you should speak with my friend who is doing great work in the space in New York," referring to Dr. Scott-Ward.

Dr. Scott-Ward was born in Brooklyn to Jamaican and Guyanese parents and realized early on that she wanted to study psychotherapy. While getting her graduate degree at Cornell University, she became curious about extracurricular courses that counted toward graduation and featured the study of hypnosis and altered states of consciousness, in part because of her own experiences with psychedelics. She realized psychedelics helped her better than the talk therapy sessions she was attending. "It enabled me to deal with my own shit," she said. She became further intrigued and took courses at MAPS, the Multidisciplinary Association for Psychedelics Studies, the Rick Doblin–founded organization that has backed MDMA studies for treating PTSD. Dr. Scott-Ward learned to incorporate her psychotherapy studies, knowledge of hypnosis and breathwork, and psychedelics into her research. I sought her out in part because of her specialization in integration, but also because of her work using both ketamine and psilocybin to help patients dealing with racial issues.

Perhaps it was the universe manifesting moves into my life, but it felt serendipitous when I had my first conversation with Gillian. In the back half of 2023, we connected virtually on several occasions to contemplate whether she would take me on as a patient.

She facilitates ketamine treatments and advises patients with varied traumas about psilocybin but cannot actually go beyond just recommending the latter as a possible treatment. Psilocybin isn't legal in New York State, where I'm licensed," she says, "so I tell my patients if they're deciding between that and ketamine, your state government has made that decision."

As far as efficacy, Gillian said both are equally proficient in dealing with trauma. "We have found that ketamine and psilocybin can regrow neurons," she said, referring to the brain cells responsible for the majority of skills, including receiving sensory input and controlling our motor skills. Those nerve cells, she said, are connected by pathways in the brain. "When we have the same thoughts and experiences and sensations over and over, the path of those experiences become worn and worn. If we're subjected to anxiety, depression, negative cognitions and beliefs, and told we're unworthy of anything and 'I feel stupid,' those become habitual and part of our core," she explained.

In my case, after several virtual sessions with Gillian, discussing my childhood in Belize, my life in the States, and my experiences throughout my career, she diagnosed me as having suffered racial trauma, which is defined as the cumulative effects of racism on an individual's mental and physical health. After hanging up following one of our last sessions and receiving that diagnosis, I hearkened back to the quote from Malcolm X that struck me so many years earlier. I had written it down several years prior but had no idea what it meant or why I had the impulse to record it. In those hours following my journey, however, it suddenly dawned on me. I had lived with the shackles of colonialism in Belize and then with the shackles of mental and cultural colonialism after I moved to the United States. I relaxed my hair with a Jheri curl and code-switched my speaking style to accommodate cultural colonialism rather than adhering to my own standards, as Malcolm X put it.

The doctor's advice: I could probably benefit from sitting with psilocybin again. "It has been shown," she said, "that by psychedelics regrowing the damaged neurons caused by racial and other forms of trauma, we can find new neural pathways, and habits can develop and this is huge." It's possible in some patients that even after one psilocybin journey, there can be considerable neural growth. "Without extra therapy, we know that psilocybin and ketamine can improve your mood, lower depression, and decrease your anxiety score, and it can last for a particular amount of time, depending on the person." The racial trauma diagnosis was a new concept to me, but because I had experienced so much healing in my previous journeys sitting with these medicines, I took the advice of Dr. Scott-Ward.

The Spiritual Underground Railroad

I had plans to be in New York City for Thanksgiving 2023 with my mom, brothers, and George. It had been weeks since my last conversation with Gillian, but it remained at the top of mind. I had learned, from a previous MSNBC producer, of a secret place called the spiritual underground railroad, a home in upstate New York just south of Albany that hosted overnight psychedelic journeys. I decided this would be the perfect moment for me to break up part of the trip ahead of the holidays, fly to Albany, and drive down to the spiritual underground. I spent more than a year having very casual conversations with the owners, Violeta and Dave, who moved permanently to the six-acre property during COVID. I had decided only the day before the retreat that I would actually do it, and as a result, I did very little research into what to expect.

I landed around noon that Friday afternoon and immediately got a text from Violeta: Don't eat anything but water after noon today, and arrive at the retreat by 5pm latest.

I thought, *Oh crap, I had a 6:00 a.m. flight this morning in coach and didn't eat anything all day.* I couldn't imagine consuming mushrooms after what, in essence, would be a twenty-four-hour fast but figured perhaps there was a reason the outward forces had brought me to central New York for this, and if it meant starvation to get the full benefit of this trip, then so be it.

As I got within two hundred yards of the spiritual underground rail station, I immediately lost cell phone service. That alone made for a traumatizing jolt to my technology addiction. I pulled up to the home—a large multistory refurbished red Dutch colonial–style house—shortly before the 5:00 p.m. arrival deadline. A white-haired hippie and a younger woman walked up to greet me.

"Hi, I'm Dave, and this is Cindy. She'll be doing the journey with you tonight."

I introduced myself and learned that Cindy was a marketing executive. Once inside, she and I sat down on two of the four yoga mats placed on the floor in front of a massive ten-foot shrine filled with candles and colorful ornaments that would have made Mahatma Gandhi proud. Violeta walked in moments later, dressed in full loose-fitting white linen clothing flowing over her body.

"Hi, honey," she said, greeting me with a big, bright smile. Violeta and Dave appeared to be in their mid-fifties. Violeta, in part because of her Latin American roots and natural spiritual intuition, had been familiar with plant medicine for some time. Dave had been running his own medical practice in Manhattan when he took a trip to South America to have his first psychedelic journey, and it turned out to be life changing. Under the spell of several different potent psychedelics, deep in the Amazon jungle, he had an out-of-body experience in which he could see himself performing surgeries, and when he made a minor error, he watched as the professional life he had built up over decades came crashing down. He took this to mean it was time to step away from practicing Western medicine. He asked, "But what next?" and within moments, through innumerable geometric figures and colors, he saw himself as a facilitator for others to experience spiritual awakenings. So, Dave closed his practice, and he and Violeta moved full-time to the Catskills just prior to COVID and opened their own home for people in need of rejuvenation and healing.

The upstate New York sun was nearly setting when Dave and Violeta returned to the tiny ten-by-ten-foot sanctuary they had constructed steps from their living room where they conducted the ceremony. They were both dressed in free-flowing white linen that signaled to me I was either about to embark on an adult baptism or be a victim in some sort of Heaven's Gate cult redux.

"Are you ready, honey?" Violeta asked. I wasn't, but I answered, "Sure thing."

"Let's get started, then." She reached over to a small metal dish from the altar, grabbed a small bundle of sage, and lit it. After circling the room with the burning sage—apparently to ward off evil spirits—she asked me to extend my arms and spread my legs as if I were being frisked by the cops (my thought, not her words, but as a Black man in America I had the procedure down pat) as she waved the bouquet around the outlines of my body. Dave then spoke:

"Now let's pray, as we look first to the east. O creator, maker of all that is and who has always been. May the rising sun remind us of who gives us great wisdom and strength. Help us, your great people, as we walk your sacred path in life, that our generations to come will have light as they walk your path. For the rays of the sun in the east, we thank you, our creator."

We turned in each direction with our hands clasped in prayer mode—the closest I'd been to any form of traditional Western religious activity in decades. Dave said the prayer was from the Lakota Native American tribe and was meant "to give gratitude for the natural world and spirit in our place." Cindy and I then sat down on the yoga mats, at opposite sides of the sanctuary site, and Dave grabbed the juice, literally. He cradled it in a fashion reminiscent of a Catholic priest holding a chalice with the "blood of Christ." As he gave me the cup, he asked what my intentions were.

"I usually don't have intentions, because in previous journeys I'll give my intentions, and the plants laugh at them and give me what *it* thinks I need instead."

"Give it to me anyway!"

"Gratitude," I said as I stared down into this silver metal cup, filled two-thirds of the way with orange juice and what looked like a lot of black pepper. Fortunately for me, it was the orange juice that was the most dominant flavor as I gulped it down. I couldn't help but notice that he placed his shrooms in orange juice just like Pulu did on that first trip in Belize and asked him if there was something to that.

"Yes, because the active form of the psilocybin is not in the mushroom; it needs your stomach acid to break it down into the next form. By grinding it up and putting it into the citric acid, it starts the digestion process in the cup, and so the effects will hit faster."

I flashed back to the white-knuckled drive on my first mushroom trip; now I realized why it kicked in much quicker than Pulu anticipated. The orange juice acts somewhat similar to the way lime does in "cooking" ceviche. At this point, I had been microdosing monthly for several years and at no point had I enquired what kind of mushrooms I was consuming or taken note of the different forms of the plant. This sparked Dave to sit down lotus-style on the far end of my mat, seemingly prepared to give me a chemistry lesson.

"There are many strains of magic mushrooms, and like everything in botany, they are divided into family, genus, and species. You just had a moderate dose of the *cubensis* species of mushrooms. They're not the strongest; they're less hallucinatory and more about giving you insights and knowledge."

"Got it," I said, relieved I wasn't given the most potent strain out there but slightly concerned by what a "moderate" dose meant, and what it would mean for me. "And what strain in the *cubensis* species did I have?" I inquired as I drank from my water bottle.

"One called albino penis envy," he responded, as I laughingly spat out some of the water in my mouth. Obviously the psychedelic world is fairly creative, and perhaps somewhat perverted in their denominations.

Fifteen minutes later, I decided to lie back and wait for the plant to kick in. Cindy immediately lay down and covered her head with a blanket once she drank her brew. Dave and Violeta both got up and grabbed various instruments to do a "sound bath," as it was called. Dave sat next to a giant Tibetan singing bowl and slowly moved a wooden mallet around the rim, creating a vibration that filled the entire room and appeared to pulse through my core. Violeta grabbed a pair of handbells that she would strike every few seconds as she moved around the room. It was fairly trippy once I closed my eyes, anticipating where the sounds were coming from. The point of the sound bath was to get everyone in the room experiencing the vibrations before the medicine really kicked in.

"They kind of stir the pot," Violeta said. "The sound churns up the essence of yourself, and the things that may come up during the ceremony." I do think there may have been something to this theory, or perhaps it was the early onset of the mushrooms. Soon, I became keenly aware of the blood flowing through the veins in my arms, hands, feet, even my face, and the sounds appeared to be guiding the flow. I concentrated on relaxing every part of my body, and I carefully regulated my breathing. Then, it began.

The Download

I immediately recognized them as I arrived. I couldn't see their faces or bodies, but I felt their energy, sensed their souls, and was aware of their anger. Despite not setting eyes on them, I knew they were holding whips, wooden paddles, even a vehicle fan belt—ironically enough, the same items that were used to discipline me and my unruly brothers when we were children in Belize. It was probably less than thirty minutes into my journey, but it already felt like it had been hours. Now, this appeared to be why I was really there.

Up to that moment, it had been the sort of psychedelic trip one would expect. The first visuals started subtly enough in a constant wave of rainbow colors that emerged suddenly from the dark canvas that was my closed eyes. Some streaked across like NBC's former public service announcement, "The More You Know," while others bathed me in a rainbow glow that reminded me of every department store window and corporate website on June 1, the start of pride month. The LGBTQ+ theme stuck around in those early moments and kept switching between the rainbow images and thoughts of my partner, George, whom at this point I had been with for nearly eleven years. My mouth started to gape as my mind tried to capture the different colors and shapes that were flying by like a time-lapse meteor shower. As much as I tried to close my mouth, I couldn't and could feel drool rolling down my lower right jaw.

Am I having a stroke? I wondered.

I had lost control of my body, and try as I might, I could not move my arms, my feet, or my shoulders to try to wipe off some of that drool that had now, much to my embarrassment, made it to my neck. Then the visuals started coming in as a recurring theme, and it was clear it had something to do with being a member of the LGBTQ+ community. The images kept flashing repeatedly with the rainbow colors—the gay pride parades I'd shunned going to, the circuit parties that I dismissed as gay Zumba because of the monotony of the beats and the mindless (mostly drugged-out) movements associated with it. It was like my brain was a computer and I was receiving downloads from a flash drive that was just inserted. There was no voice in my head like I'd had with ayahuasca, which ended up being my inner soul, but instead the message here came through the visuals, and it appeared to be telling me to lean into my bisexuality.

An image in a giant font scrolled across, asking:

"Why aren't there more images of me and George on my social media?"

I thought, *Because I'm trying to keep my options open. Also, I don't feature Tito on my page either; they have their own pages.* I was slightly defensive. It kept hammering home images indicating I may be embarrassed of being in a long-term gay relationship and didn't show George enough love. It was so repeated and clear, it was as if George had secretly met with Dave to create some wild secret magic mushroom formula that would reflect some of *his* thoughts and feelings. Perhaps the psychedelic version of sticking pins and needles into a voodoo doll. It's amazing what your mind accepts as absolutely factual when rolling on mushrooms.

I began to breathe heavily through my mouth, making a loud blowing sound with each exhale in a gesture reminiscent of the ceremony in the Peruvian Amazon. I still couldn't move, but I felt the sensations all throughout my body while my core temperature vacillated between overheated sweating and shivering cold. Depending on how I reacted, Violeta added or removed a blanket from on top of me. The visuals moved so rapidly back and forth across my mind's spectrum, my head began to rock from side to side, giving the appearance of someone short-circuiting. I watched the pride flags morph into a rainbow, then suddenly, my torso lifted up and I was jolted awake into the sitting position. I looked around the room, which was now dark. The ceiling was filled with stars from a light or some sort of effect Dave and Violeta turned on while my eyes were closed. Cindy had not moved; she remained in the same position as before with the blanket covering her face. Violeta walked over to me, kneeled down, smoked some sort of tobacco, and blew the exhaust around my face.

"Are you okay, honey?"

"Yeah, I am. It's just a lot." I felt higher than I'd ever been in my life, and that was really saying something given my previous experiences. I knew I wanted to throw up. I grabbed the tiny bucket off to the right of my mat, cradled it in my legs folded in the lotus position, and spat a few times while breathing heavily. Violeta poured something that smelled like witch hazel in her hand and asked me to inhale deeply a few times, which I did, and it calmed my rapid heartbeat and nerves for a bit.

"It's just a lot coming at me right now, but I get it," I told her, but I was also telling the medicine that as well. I recalled Katya in Arizona telling me that if it gets to be too much, speak to the medicine and ask it to ease up, which I did here, and enjoyed a brief respite before the brain circuitry rebooted and was ready to download more. I lay back down on the mat and covered myself with the blanket. As I closed my eyes again, the pride parade subsided, and I said to the plant, "Thank you."

A Remarkable Shift

The drug took on an increasingly physical component as my arms started to twitch in a rhythm synchronized to the visuals. Suddenly, everything went to black; there were no more streaks, no rainbows, no pride flags, no eggplant emojis flying across my screen. My body was definitely not my own from that moment going forward. My twitching arms started banging harder into the side of my thighs. I became incredibly uncomfortable in my skin and clothes and started shedding the blanket on top of me and removing a veil-thin sweatshirt I was wearing over a tank top. I switched and moved my head to the opposite end of the mat.

That'll do it, I thought. But it didn't.

I flipped my body from lying on my right side, and then quickly onto my left side, and back again. There was no getting comfortable with this.

Man, I feel high AF.

The canvas in my brain remained dark and blank without any prevailing visuals. I sat up impulsively with the urge to throw up. I searched around for the tiny bowl and noticed the room had gone intensely darker. Violeta had departed the room, but I could see Dave on the far end of the sanctuary, or a figure I thought was Dave. It was hard to make sense of what I was seeing. I saw this figure in long white overalls, and where I would have normally expected to see one human head, there were three. That object walked toward me, and with every step, all I saw was a distortion that featured three different bodies, and so many distorted colors were plastered onto what should have been the face, it appeared like I'd gone to drag queen heaven—or hell, actually.

"Hey, brotha, I just want you to know you're doing a great job."

"Thanks. I feel really high right now."

"Just know it goes through waves. Just relax and let it do what it needs to do," he reassured me. I was fairly sure that even if I relaxed, the plant would do whatever it wanted with my body. I lay back down on the mat, took his advice, and capitulated. I spoke to the plant and said, *I give in. Go ahead and do whatever you'd like.*

I assume it had been about an hour since I first received the drink, and based on the guidance from Violeta before we got started, the truly intense portions of this would likely last up to four hours. Despite me giving in to the plant, I didn't feel too many body twitches or see many visuals once I lay there.

Is it over? Was that the only thing I needed to download? I needed to embrace being a bisexual person more publicly and like George more? If that's it, then I got the lesson. How 'bout I just get up?

With ayahuasca, after I received the message the tea wanted me to have, I felt that I was in control of my capacities and wondered if perhaps this was the case here. I stood up to go to the bathroom, stumbled, and did a face-plant onto the other mat to my left. I looked over at Cindy, who had not made any sort of noises, wasn't moving, didn't breathe heavily, and didn't appear to have gotten the same drink. I didn't understand how anyone could have taken that potion and not felt like they went on a psychedelic roller coaster. The mind goes to wild places on psychedelics, and at that moment, mine wondered whether Cindy was actually given anything and if I was there as part of some weird séance about to be sacrificed. Violeta told me later, "Often people will just lie there like a corpse for three to four hours. They're not moving muscles or anything, and we make sure they're breathing."

Dave grabbed my arm and helped me get upright, and I wobbled outside the room to a nearby bathroom to pee, making sure not to look into the mirror. If I thought I had self-esteem and body dysmorphia issues before, I couldn't imagine the goblin I would have noticed at that moment.

I lay back down on my stomach with my head to the right, and suddenly, there they were: every person I knew who had passed away. My aunt, Ms. Jerry (one of my mother's best friends), my dad, my grandmother, who was named Aunt Nora (confusing, I know), and a host of others lined up too far behind for me to be able to tell who they were, but I knew they were family members. My aunt had just passed two months prior and I delivered her eulogy, and Ms. Jerry died earlier in 2023. It seemed as if the lineup depended on who had transitioned most recently; my dad, who died in 2005, was positioned in the third row behind some close cousins.

I wondered: *I asked for gratitude when I made intentions. What the hell are they all doing here?*

As soon as I saw them, or rather felt their energy, my right hand started slamming into my thigh, again, and again, and over again, and increasingly harder. The images began to unload rapidly, and my face, which was pressed against the pillow, started to swivel up and down.

I had an out-of-body experience in which I flew out of my core being and traveled back in time. I observed like a fly on the wall of my life the thousands of times I had pressed my nose together to make it look more Anglo. I watched myself look at White boys in the locker room when I first moved to the United States and felt the emotions I experienced looking at them with envy, admiration, and idolization. I saw a thirteen-year-old me having that horribly painful elective circumcision. My feet got into the action by repeatedly rubbing the heel of my left foot against the arc at the top of my right foot. This continued so frequently and harshly, my heel eventually rubbed the skin from the top of my foot raw and caused it to turn my white sock bloody from the exposed wound. I got back up and flipped sides again. Mind you I wasn't in control of this action. I just kept thinking, *This is a powerful drug.*

I was getting a lot of information, but it wasn't clear yet what the message was. The elders remained to the right of my shoulder, and while their energy wasn't moving, I knew they were directing this assault, and I did not like it one bit. I opened my eyes and sat up and scrambled around for the barf bowl. Luckily, Dave came over with the bowl just in time for me to spit a few times, but shockingly there was no puke. Everyone purges in their own way, whether it is shitting, crying, peeing, or sweating. Mine seemed to have been throwing up.

"Can I get you anything?"

Yeah, get this fucking thing out of me. I'm way too high and it's too much.

"It's okay; it's just a lot. A lot of information coming at me, Dave."

"You're doing great, buddy. Would you want to walk outside and get some cool air?"

"Sure."

I walked outside, wearing a tank top and thin, loose-fitting pajama pants on what was a typical fall night in the Catskills, with the temperatures in the lower thirties, and it was the most refreshing thing I could have imagined. I still didn't know what to make of the images and physical actions that were taking place. I looked up and stretched out my arms into the sky, and suddenly, it began to snow lightly. I could feel every flake as it touched my face, lowering my body temperature with each contact. In that moment, it felt like I had summoned that snowfall out of nowhere, and that in turn made me feel empowered to handle whatever was waiting for me in the sanctuary.

After cooling down for a few minutes, I walked back into the room and assumed the same position as before. Nearly immediately, the pounding returned, with my arms banging back and forth and the presence of my "loved" ones on my shoulder. The screen in my mind turned to the whitening cream I'd used when I was younger to lighten my skin. It showed that cream as it squeezed out of a bottle and turned into a snakelike creature as it reached my face, which I rubbed all around.

The plant clearly knew I hated snakes and used this imagery to hammer home a point. It showed me pictures of the myriad White men and women I'd lusted after and wished I could be, and it morphed their bodies into rotting corpses and, in some cases, showed how they spoke about me in a degrading manner behind my back. My television career flashed across my mental screen, and showed how I had spent the entire time shunning my Blackness and not fighting for other BIPOC colleagues throughout my career. I saw myself in the boardroom with the executives and Barbara Fedida at the opposite end of the table from me and morphed her into a snake that grew in size and stretched over to my end of the table and swallowed me, while the headline featured her words: "ABC spends more on toilet paper than we ever would on him." I was quickly transported to my childhood home, the one with the outhouse in the front yard, and Fedida's words somehow combined with that imagery and my face turned into the toilet paper that was used in that outhouse that wiped someone's ass.

What does all this mean?

Next, I saw my mom dealing with colonial British soldiers from the moment she was a child in Belize, soldiers who spat on her and diminished her worth. Then I saw her watching Princess Margaret and idolizing her beauty. I heard the elders who spoke in one voice even though it was coming from so many of my ancestors. They proclaimed, "By idolizing the White colonialist lifestyle and White concept of beauty, your mom was trying to protect you from the hate that exists in this world, whether it's colonial racist Belize or traditional racist American culture."

My ancestors showed me as a god, and then a goddess. I have suffered body dysmorphia my entire life, never appreciating my body, my abs, or my ass, and was a perennial dieter. My long-gone relatives now showed me my body and features as Black as they were centuries ago, and it was the most beautiful thing I had ever seen. I flew from outer space as a comet and broke off as a speck of its tail that came to earth and landed in Ghana, which a DNA test later showed me the majority of my people came from, and I was dancing with tribes. I was enjoying my people, and my rhythm, my nose, and my ass were extraordinary—they were great.

The mental download was coming in fast, thorough, and with repetition. I suddenly saw myself as the sexiest, Blackest goddess imaginable. My body twisted to attenuate all my curves, and my hands rubbed over my nose, my fat lips, and down to my big Black ass and thick legs in loving, proud, and appreciative fashion. I've never enjoyed myself as much as I did at that moment.

And suddenly, it all stopped and went to a blank white space in my mind. My loved ones remained to the right of my shoulder, but the physical and mental whipping they choreographed had subsided. I lay on my back on the mat, bathed in a warm glow surrounding my body, and even with my eyes closed, I could see how bright this was. The light assured me of my worth as a Black man, and despite the decades of trauma I experienced through colonialism, American society, and television network culture, I knew I was part of a much, much greater plan far beyond anything I could have imagined. And for the first time ever, I felt that to my core, in my bones, and running through every vein. It was remarkable.

Healing on the Mountain

I opened my eyes. "Wow!" I said as I stared at the ceiling with starry lights placed there by an effect Dave and Violeta did during the journey. I slowly sat up and looked around the room. Everything was blurry, but for the first time I could remember, Cindy was moving. She got off her mat and appeared to be solving some sort of puzzle swiveling around two of the puke bowls, then performing a half push-up and then repeating. And then she did the strangest thing I've ever seen. She flipped her body backward, with her face looking toward the ground, as she walked on all fours up the small set of steps that connected the sanctuary to the living room and the rest of the house, à la *The Ring*. I was in no position to judge, in part because I was still high, and I was completely convinced I had just flown through space and time and communicated with my loved ones who had passed many years ago. I was exhausted, bloodied, and sore and needed time to assess this experience. It was definitely not what I had anticipated when I first sat down on that mat and gave my intention, but I knew the thing that called me there had to do with my self-image. While ayahuasca taught me to love myself, this wanted me to know my self-worth.

I didn't sleep much that night. Violeta gave me the entire basement apartment, which consisted of a full kitchen, two bedrooms, living space, and even my own outdoor patio. I was bruised, mentally and emotionally, and I was too shaken to sleep. It took nine hours from when I drank the mushroom concoction to when I finally felt that it had flushed its way out of my system along with most of the hallucinogenic effects.

But then I had to grapple with all that the medicine wanted me to know, and it's those lessons that kept my mind racing for several hours longer. My right arm was sore, as if I had done a biceps workout the day before, and my shoulder where my ancestors sat for the majority of the night was tingling, even though that area was not physically stimulated at all during the journey. The top of my right foot had been rubbed raw by the heel of my left foot and soaked my sock with blood. (Note to self: prior to my next psychedelic journey, get a pedicure and a smoothing scrub on my heels beforehand.) There was no part of that psychedelic experience that I enjoyed. It was a first for me. I always associated mushrooms with flipping on a light switch on life, making everything brighter and building an appreciation for the smallest things and, more importantly, for being alive. It is why Violeta and Dave insist their guests spend the night following a journey. In the past, Dave was forced to block the driveway with his car, because many guests believed they were sober enough to drive and tried to leave for the night. He would do that in part to make sure people wouldn't drive while the effects of the medicine were still being felt but also because of what needs to happen the morning following a journey: the integration. "We don't want anyone rushing out of here fighting demons," said Violeta.

I searched online to find there's no set parameters on the way the integration is handled, which is simply defined as the "period following a psychedelic experience." I understood its importance, and I felt there was a lot I needed to reconcile.

I didn't eat much the night before, so I was looking forward to the big breakfast Violeta promised. By the time I got upstairs, the table was made, coffee was ready, and eggs from their own hens were scrambled and set on the table. It was a large, healthy meal filled with fruits and vegetables that were all cultivated on their property, and everything left over was returned to the earth and animals; nothing was wasted. It was strange sitting next to Cindy at breakfast, as the last time I saw her, she had been "dead" for the majority of the evening, and then was solving puzzles with the puke buckets, and finally had flipped her body backward and crawled out of the room, seemingly back to the well from *The Ring*.

"Are you okay?" I asked her.

"Yeah, why?"

So, I guess I'm the only one who saw that crazy shit last night from her?

"Aw, no reason. Just wanted to make sure you were good."

Violeta, Dave, Cindy, and I all sat down around a table facing their two-story fireplace. Dave got us started:

"We will just go around the room, and you can share as much as you feel comfortable doing. It is meant to ground yourself following the medicine."

Violeta chimed in, " You may have some contractions, where for no particular reasons you'll have some aha moments, some expansive thoughts, as you integrate the medicine into your life over the next few days and weeks."

Cindy went first in describing her journey, which apparently reverted her to her childhood and not feeling nurtured and loved enough by her mom. The blanket that she kept over her face for the majority of the trip made her feel like she was back in the womb and was protected and safe. And then when she finally emerged from the womb, she was solving puzzles because that was her as a child playing games with her friends. I leaned in, hoping that she would then explain why the hell she turned into Sadako Yamamura from *The Ring*, but that answer never surfaced.

"There was a lot of bodywork for you, Kendis," Dave said. "There was clearly a fight, and your body was kind of mirroring what's going on inside."

"You were working some stuff out," Violeta added.

I told the group about the initial download I received from the plant involving pride in my sexuality and an appreciation for who I am and who I have in my life who are loving me. I also mentioned my ancestors were there with plenty of whips and belts to crack me into shape.

"I could totally see that," Violetta said. "Usually with people you can tell when a message is sent, and that person receives it and then their body reactions change. You kept doing the same bodily functions, as if your ancestors believed you were not understanding what they were saying and they wouldn't let up until you did." They certainly did not.

In the hours following the journey, I was able to reexamine what they were trying to reinforce in me, and it definitely was about knowing and having pride in myself as a Black man in this world, who comes from a line of amazing, enlightened, beautiful people. I had shunned that for the majority of my life. When I finally stood up at ABC News and helped to fight for diversity behind the scenes, it wasn't because I thought it was to benefit my own people but because I thought it would benefit my White executives at the network. I had spent my entire broadcast career cultivating relationships and friendships with White bosses and believed that we operated in a post-racial society and industry. At ABC News, I would have drinks with plenty of the executives who were in the rooms when some of the most horrid conversations regarding myself were taking place. When I took the baton to lead those diversity meetings, I believed the White executives would view me as someone with a genuine interest in making the network better and helping their bottom line. Which is why the ABC News revelations about Barbara Fedida's feelings and words toward me were so much more damaging than anything else I had experienced in my life; it upended my entire being. Not only was I just a regular "nigger," my value was worth less than what "we" as White network people would wipe their asses with. It wasn't until I was called to do this mushroom journey that I realized there was unfinished business in my head mentally, and I gained the full context of what I had done my entire life and what I needed to do to fix it going forward. While I initially took all the colors at the outset to indicate I needed to focus on LGBTQ+ pride, Violeta said I should look beyond that surface meaning. "If you experience rainbows in the psychedelic world, it means enlightenment."

My intention for this trip was "gratitude," and while technically I didn't achieve that, I did gain an appreciation for my relationships, my sexuality, my culture, my ancestors, my Blackness, and most importantly, my self-worth.

After little more than an hour of discussing and sitting with the lessons of the medicine, we wrapped with a prayer:

"Let's thank all the angels, the spirit guides, the ascended masters, our creator, our ancestors, all of those who showed up last night, who protected and who also showed the way. We take this information to try to make ourselves and humanity better, and we now close this space. Thank you to all those who showed up."

We all hugged, thanked each other, and promised to continue our integration together as we went about our lives.

After saying our goodbyes, I left, and after five minutes on the road, my cell phone signal returned and suddenly downloaded the dozens of messages I'd missed while up on the mountain. I smiled as the notifications rolled in, put the phone away for a few minutes, and looked at the road ahead while I reflected on the life-changing insights I'd received in the previous eighteen hours. Violeta was correct about those rainbows—I was enlightened.

Epilogue

Am I cured? Who knows? It'll be an ongoing and evolving story. I received this checklist from Dr. Scott-Ward that helps guide me through my days:

- Do I have practices and community and lifestyle that allow me to feel safe and grounded and protected? Check.
- Do I feel like I have ownership and agency over what happens in my life and what goes on in my world? Check.

"If you can maintain connection to those foundational experiences and beliefs," says Scott-Ward, "then it's a great way to start each day and maintain sanity and grounding with your world."

At times, based on the ass-whooping I received during some of these journeys, it felt like I was doing a psychedelic version of *Super Size Me*, the 2004 documentary in which Morgan Spurlock put his mind and body on the line by eating only fast food for a month and recording what it did to him. In the end, for all the revelatory healing that I experienced, I still had plenty of questions. For example, why did MDMA help me come to terms with childhood sexual abuse and the PTSD of the death of my first childhood crush? Why did a certain strain of psilocybin seem to improve my panic attacks? Why did

I need ayahuasca to teach me self-love and to be able to appreciate myself and help calm my lifelong suicidal ideation?

Finally, I wondered: *Was it the chemical makeup in these varied psychedelics—ayahuasca, MDMA, and psilocybin—that brought me to a place where I could handle my trauma and live a happier life?* The response from a Cornell-trained medical professional floored me. "It wasn't the science," she said, and that had me reexamining everything I learned from these five trips, the numerous professionals I'd spoken with, and my entire life journey.

I wanted to know the science behind it, and I felt it was important for me to get those answers from the top Black and Brown doctors and experts in the field. While many pointed to different charts that showed increased brain activity and research studies that indicated improvement in people's behavior, there was one common refrain from all these well-respected Western medically trained professionals: why plant medicine works has as much to do with spirituality as it does with science. However, Dr. Scott-Ward cautions, "Until it becomes legalized, we need to focus on the scientific, the concrete, and steer away from the spiritual aspect," adding with a smile, "But when I think about my own experience, I got to connect with my ancestors."

If you do an online search to define "spirituality," you'll get a lot of answers, but one definition I found really spoke to me: "You do not know precisely what is happening or exactly where it is all going. What you need is to recognize the possibilities and challenges offered by the present moment and to embrace them with courage, faith, and hope." That's exactly how I feel.

In hindsight, this journey didn't begin in the fall of 2020 when I started writing this book, or earlier in the year when I did mushrooms with Pulu, nor was it in the early 2000s when I first discovered the impact of MDMA. I've come to believe it was predetermined. I was meant to be alive following that fall from the bedroom window while I was a newborn, survive childhood sexual abuse and trauma, beat poverty, persevere through racism on various levels, and persist—despite my deep depression—so that I could have this spiritual awakening and connect with my ancestors, whether it was on top of that ruin in Caracol, or the sighting by the shaman of my deceased dad and nephew while I did ayahuasca in Peru, or their tough-love presence at the spiritual underground railroad.

This wasn't just a journey to write a book that could help others. It was a spiritual awakening to help *me*.

I've found myself deeply and profoundly changed since these journeys. I often wonder what took me so long to make these discoveries and if I would have been more financially successful earlier, would have been hosting *GMA*, or would have had a healthier life where I wasn't abusing alcohol and prescription pills. I'll never know. I do feel that I needed to experience all those dark days and nights, those career speed bumps and health scares, to have gained the knowledge and immense appreciation of my own life, and to value more the people dearest to me. I am happier, I have a healthier relationship with alcohol, and, most importantly, I live a life of gratitude. So much so, I became receptive to returning to television news, and did so in spring 2024 as weekday anchor for WPIX, the powerhouse local independent television station that I also grew up watching as a teenager in the Big Apple. I was back home, in New York, and on television. It felt like a homecoming in more ways than one.

Acknowledgments

I'd like to thank everyone who ever responded to my texts, reached out to call, checked up on me, or expressed their concerns during the darkest times in my mental health struggles, including Diane Macedo, Mara S. Campo, Robyn Love, Bryan Keinz, Mike Woods, Tom Morgan, Glenn Rink, Marc Davis, Susan Lennon, Kathleen Bade, Yetta Gibson, Lisa Bonner, Nekisha Mohan, James Duran, Jawn Murray, Yolanda Johnson, Britt Mchenry, Eddie Roche, Scott Stachowiak, and Rick Reichmuth.

Special thanks to those who reinforced the importance of telling my story, including James Boyd, Nikki Steward, Christine Choi, Shyne Barrow, Sunny Hostin, Kimani Bunch, Shaun Francis, and Michael Strahan.

Big thanks to those who got me started on this magical journey discovering plant medicine: Pulu Lightburn and Clay Brown. The Johntourage: Matt Gasiorowski, John Masse, Jevon Hicks.

Drew Brody, thank you so much for lending your talents to the manuscript. Lori Tharps, your support and guidance through this project were immeasurable. Mark Leibowitz, you're such an amazing photographer and a better friend. Thank you for your incredible work with the book covers. Jennifer Campanile, Paula Madison, and Trent Copeland, you make an amazing team. Fatima and Don, I truly believe there's a reason the universe brought us into each other's lives.

Prince Ghuman, thank you for agreeing to jump on a plane with two weeks' notice and head to the Amazon with me to experience our life-changing ayahuasca experience and bonding.

Much gratitude to the amazing contributors who gave me their time and immeasurable knowledge, Dr. Joseph Mccowan, Dr. Stephanie Michael Stewart, Dr. Gillian Scott-Ward, William Padilla-Brown, and Gabi Curandeira.

George P. Brown III, your patience and love know no bounds. Thanks for the support of my in-laws, George P. Brown II and Diane Brown.

Special love and thanks to my brothers: thank you for being there throughout.

Special mention to Marvin Gibson, Brian Gibson, Aldoray Gibson, Dean Gibson, and Alrick Gibson Jr.

And to my parents, without whom none of this journey would be possible: Alrick and Hortense Gibson.

About the Author

Kendis Gibson *is a four-time Emmy Award–winning journalist. Over his decades-long career, Gibson has covered some of the biggest stories impacting our world. He was one of the first journalists to Ground Zero following the terrorist attacks on 9/11, escaping only minutes before the first tower fell.*